Date Due

SOLDIER TO CIVILIAN

SOLDIER TO CIVILIAN

Problems of Readjustment

BY

GEORGE K. PRATT, M.D.

Psychiatric Examiner, U. S. Armed Forces, Induction Center,
New Haven, Connecticut; formerly Assistant Clinical
Professor of Psychiatry, School of Medicine,
Yale University

Foreword by

GEORGE S. STEVENSON, M.D.

Medical Director, The National Committee for
Mental Hygiene

WHITTLESEY HOUSE

MC GRAW-HILL BOOK COMPANY, INC.

New York   *London*

SOLDIER TO CIVILIAN

Copyright, 1944, by the McGraw-Hill Book Company, Inc.

This book is produced in full compliance with the government's regulations for conserving paper and other essential materials.

PUBLISHED BY WHITTLESEY HOUSE
A division of the McGraw-Hill Book Company, Inc.

Printed in the United States of America

DEDICATED TO

My son Cpl. Rodney G. Pratt who is
with the Army Signal Corps overseas

CONTENTS

FOREWORD

THE rising value of human life in America is one of the signs of our advancing culture. The evidence of its existence is all about us and it needs no argument. But the value of human living as contrasted with human life is not yet on a sound standard, although public health, education, theology, medicine, and social work have been expanding their interests in morbidity, mortality, and casualties to encompass the more positive satisfying, effective, and productive living. Their services are more and more measured by how well their beneficiaries live instead of by patterns of action born of tradition or authority.

During the depression of 1929 man-days were cheap, and, paradoxically, it has taken a period of apparent inhumanity, of war, to bring home to us the value of human living as expressed by man power. But still this is too often seen as a value to a society or nation, an imaginary being transcending its members, rather than to and through them exclusively. Yet it is not strange that out of a way of life and a political system known as democracy should come, through whatever portal, a welcome concern for the value of people. If man is worth salvaging he is worth it for himself. No other justification is needed. He was just as needful of satisfactions in 1932 as in 1942. Shall the services that surround him now be allowed to decline? We think not. Out of this materialistic, inhumanitarian, and entirely opportunistic impulse has come a deeply humanitarian and farsighted program. The rehabilitation of returning veterans will save us money, pangs of guilt, demagoguery, crime, poverty-stricken families, and disease, and yet without these savings it would be justified if it gave the veteran his appropriate opportunity in our national life and put the seal of approval on a national policy of respect for the importance of the individual.

An attempt is made in the pages that follow to show how reasonable are the quandaries of the veteran, considering what he has been through and how reasonable it is that we should not throw the whole burden of finding his way upon shoulders that are new to this type of responsibility, nor take from those shoulders loads that they can carry. It is not a matter of rewarding a man for work well done. Veterans are not asking that, although they are not beyond enticement into it. The veteran needs retooling. It is retooling for effective civilian living just as he was previously retooled for effective military living. Many gratuities, such as pensions, may be thrown to him that will have an opposite effect. For example, the GI Bill of Rights—in many respects an admirable measure—is very much a bill of rewards. Among the provisions, it "rewards" the deserter, the criminal, the fraudulently enlisted, and the undesirable character with "rights" that will frequently contribute to his failure. For the well balanced the reward becomes an incentive to action. For others it may become an incentive to dependence. Bonuses of a new style are needed—bonuses that "pay the debt of disability in the currency of opportunity." Such bonuses are as much harder to administer as they are more effective and are correspondingly easy to mishandle. They require biological and psychiatric as well as political thinking, for to be effective they must enhance life first of all, rather than prestige and power. Perhaps the need is summed up in the words "social statesmanship."

What is done wisely or unwisely for the veteran will be a sign and measure of our times and a forecast of our future. The veteran is humanity of the moment. Tomorrow he will be a part of our rural, town, and city life again and a heavy participant in our government. What we do for him will tell us and him where we stand in the 1940's. It will give him and us the cue for plans ahead. It will set the pace for services and considerations for our whole population. If we act intelligently now, we do so for many years to come.

This is a task for our whole public. Nothing could do more to strengthen democracy than universal participation in meeting this kind of reality with the same energy and time as we applied to air-raid precautions. But the task is to no small degree technical, and, if sound processes are to be effected, processes that will result in success of this broad effort rather than the disillusionment that follows superficial dabbling, a professional personnel well selected and trained is essential. It is a task as well for a variety of professions and trades. The needs of the veteran will most frequently be nothing more than a friendly, loving, receptive public ready to give the veteran the opportunity to resume civilian life. In many instances there will be needs for more specialized help, medical for the disabled, occupational guidance for the young and handicapped, social services for the shattered family, educational service for those requiring retraining or continuance of plans, and financial help for a variety of circumstances. How can those who are able to be of service become known to the veteran who needs the service? How can he be encouraged to use the service and still to use to the utmost his own resources? How can new services be developed to meet his needs? How can they be continually tested to measure their value and effectiveness? These are the practical questions whose answers in large part are still ahead of us if we have the soundness and humility that are essential to progress. The pages that follow give the spirit and direction for the next years wherewith to transform into practical social action a principle that we have fought to establish as our political safeguard.

—GEORGE S. STEVENSON, M.D.
Medical Director,
The National Committee for Mental Hygiene

1

INTRODUCTION

THIS book deals with some of the problems of adjusting to family and community life faced by the returned soldier or sailor. Since the war is not ended as the book is written virtually all of the men it concerns up to date have been discharged from military service because of some type of handicap, either physical or psychological. Nevertheless, many of the problems of community adjustment faced by discharged men are identical with the problems to be faced by millions of others who will be demobilized at the close of the war. Thus, the book may prove helpful in understanding the difficulties of adaptation to civilian life of both groups.

It is addressed primarily to the families, friends, and prospective employers of all returned servicemen, and its purpose is to create in these families and others both a point of view and an atmosphere. The point of view is one of mature, not mawkish, sympathy. The atmosphere, it is hoped, may become one of understanding and sturdy support, in which the man in whom they are interested may be helped to help himself in establishing on his return home ways of living that will prove satisfying to him and effective for good citizenship. But there are grave dangers to the man himself no less than to the future of the nation as a whole if families and others fail to understand his problems and thereby fail to help him achieve a normal civilian life. Suppose we see how one family with excellent intentions hindered rather than helped their son in his efforts to adjust after returning home.

The Arthur Stones [1] were typical New England citizens properly proud of their twenty-year-old son Arthur, Jr., who had been with a tank corps outfit in Tunisia, at Salerno, and in Anzio. His previous good luck deserted him in the battle for Florence, when vicious pieces of mortar fragments sliced across his neck and face and for a time rendered him unconscious.

After months in a succession of hospitals, where he received the most highly skilled medical attention any human being could hope for, Arthur was shipped back to the States and given a discharge. He really was feeling pretty hale and hearty by this time and had just about conquered his first feelings of sick despair when he saw his facial disfigurement in the mirror. The psychiatrist at the last convalescent hospital had talked quite a bit to Arthur about the psychological effects of his injuries, and the boy consequently had lost most of his oversensitiveness and morbid preoccupation with them. Now there were whole days at a time when he never thought any longer about his face, and he rapidly found himself on the road to think-

[1] All names of persons as used in case-histories in this book are fictitious.

ing of himself as not different from anyone else. He was excited and happy at prospects of returning home and already had made dozens of plans about what he would do when he got back.

As Arthur stepped from the train Mother, Dad, and young brother Eddie waved a greeting and rushed toward him. His face broke into what he meant for a grin of pleasure but actually it was a twisted, grotesque grimace from severed muscles that would not properly behave. Although the boy had written them a general account of his wounds Mr. and Mrs. Stone weren't prepared for this, and instinctively they recoiled at what they saw. Their shock was not concealed, and Arthur's heightened sensitivity caused him to read revulsion into it. But the Stones quickly recovered. With nervous, high-pitched chatter to cover their agitation they took Arthur home.

To the returned soldier the next few weeks were almost worse than the battlefield. Having made gains toward thinking of himself as a fairly normal individual and wanting others to treat him as one he found the forced joviality of the family and their artificial Pollyanna-like treatment both unrealistic and irritating. It annoyed him beyond words to have Mother tiptoe about the house, shushing everyone who talked loudly, to have her fuss over him and to see the tears of silent pity course down her cheeks as she begged him to "rest" on the couch in the living room. He felt like screaming when he overheard snatches of muted telephone conversations behind closed doors with repeated references to "poor Arthur." He strove manfully to stifle his exasperation when his mother insisted on his reciting over and over again the intimate details of his wounding; how it happened; did it hurt much; did he lose quantities of blood; were the doctors and nurses good to him; how did it feel to be under enemy fire; was he frightened; did he think to pray, etc., etc., until her well-meaning interrogations into these personal matters hurt worse than the surgeon's probing for embedded mortar fragments. To Arthur these things were private; not even a mother had a right to drag them out into the open. Moreover, she looked hurt when he answered some of her questions with "I don't remember." Mrs. Stone thought her son was deliberately trying to conceal horrors from her. She didn't know that Arthur's "I don't remember" was the plain truth; that he had been temporarily knocked unconscious and that in addition he—like thousands of other soldiers in combat—automatically developed a protective amnesia or loss of memory to blot out the more ghastly part of his experience. His insistence that he failed to remember was not a deliberate white lie to spare her feelings. He honestly didn't recall many of the details into which she probed.

Even Dad with all his good intentions was scarcely less irritating. He had been in the Argonne in World War I, and his prestige as the sole military expert of the family had been unchallenged until this son of his likewise achieved the status of a veteran. Mr. Stone loved his son dearly but at the same time he now felt threatened by Arthur's competition. And so it happened that each time Arthur recounted some incident of the battlefield his father found it necessary to match it with an incident of his own, always contriving to make *his* experience a little more exciting. At first Arthur didn't mind, but as Dad reminisced incessantly the boy grew irked. After all, his father had had his day; Arthur was the returning hero now, and he didn't relish being relegated once more to the position of second fiddle. Then, too, there were the arguments on topics about which Arthur held some positive ideas of his own. Mr. Stone, for instance, hadn't liked sergeants in his war, and he reviled them bitterly, endeavoring to get his son to agree with him. But Sergeant Donovan had been Arthur's best friend; indeed, he was the one who dragged the boy to shelter when he had been hit, and Arthur couldn't see things his father's way. The arguments waxed furiously and spread to other topics until both were angry and upset. Mr. Stone didn't know about Sergeant Donovan, and as his son grew more hostile the father's arguments became more heated and repetitious.

The thing that infuriated the returned soldier most of all, however, was his parents' resumption of the old attitude, "Mother and Dad know best," used so lovingly but firmly all during his boyhood. Up to his entrance into the army "Mother and Dad know best" had been the customary and clinching restraining force on those adolescent plans with which they disagreed. On his return Mr. and Mrs. Stone failed to realize that this soldier son of theirs was little Arthur no longer. They couldn't realize that he had become accustomed to making and executing his own plans for two years and that sometimes his very life had depended on their soundness. On his return home it was natural but unwise for his parents to slip into the old habit of countering his ideas with this phrase, but to Arthur it grew increasingly irritating. When he announced that he was going down to the corner drugstore to hunt up some of the old crowd, and when Mother gently suggested he had better stay home on the couch and rest, the ensuing argument ended as of yore with "But we know best, dear." When Arthur, who had figured out the situation for himself, told the family that he wasn't going to try to get his old job back but seek another, the same parental words were invoked in opposition.

All in all, Arthur began to feel that his homecoming was a letdown. Day by day and week by week the atmosphere at home created by the family insidiously sapped the desire for independence and normality of the returned soldier. He had reached home after bitter struggles within himself, beginning to feel sturdy and of a likeness with others, full of fresh young plans for himself, invigorated and enthusiastic. But the family treated him not only like an invalid from whom little should be expected, but as the same happy-go-lucky kid he was before the war; as one who didn't know his own mind and whose youthful enthusiasms were to be received with amused tolerance but no seriousness. Gradually, his desire for independence weakened. Gradually, he began to take over into himself their concept of him as an invalid, and gradually he slipped back imperceptibly into his former status of "little Arthur" until his new-found inner urgings for a normal place in the world were stifled and abandoned.

This family approached their son's problems harmfully, although they did not mean to, because they failed to understand what it was he wanted on his return and how he felt about matters that to him were vitally important. As a result his return to a successful civilian adjustment was needlessly impeded.

The soldier home from the wars will seem a curious bundle of contradictions to his family. In some areas of his life military experience will have matured him. In others he will appear downright childish. He will want freedom from military discipline and at the same time feel bewildered to know what to do with his new civilian liberty. He will express a wish for social activities and yet feel uneasy when these are provided. He will talk much of craving to settle down into humdrum routine and security and yet in a few weeks yearn restlessly for change and to be once more on the go. Most of all however, the returned soldier will be *different*—different in hundreds of little ways from the man his family knew before he went away; different in his outlook on life; different in his manner of doing things; different in his sense of values; different in his likes and dislikes. In brief, he is apt to seem for a time almost a stranger to his puzzled family.

It is at this point that he needs understanding, but even more he needs to come back to a home atmosphere, a community atmosphere, a job atmosphere that will interpose no obstacles to his task of refinding himself, an atmosphere that will accept him for what he is and permit him to work out his own problems in his own way. You and I may honestly believe that we know what is best for him and we may try lovingly to shape him into a mold of our selection, but he is likely to have other ideas. Some of his ideas will prove sound, others not. Some will meet our approval, but others may disturb us. The point is that he will have to be permitted to embark on one of the most exciting—and sometimes most dangerous—of all life's adventures: trial and error in living. In so doing he is bound now and then to come a cropper in which he, and possibly others, too, will be hurt. But you and

I cannot (or at least we should not) wholly prevent this. He must learn for himself, and if in the process he stubs his toe let us keep discreet silence and allow him to chalk up the injury to experience.

This trial-and-error process can be shortened and its errors made less painful if we can provide the returned soldier with the climate of understanding mentioned above. In such a climate he will find freedom to grow in maturity, although perhaps after his own fashion; he will come to sense in us a quality of true understanding and steadfastness on which he can depend, even at those times when his inner confusion and illogical resentments are greatest. He will derive a sense of support from his intuitive realization that we do, after all, have comprehension of the struggles he is going through inside himself and that while we may not always approve of what he does, yet we neither condemn nor reject him for doing it. Such an atmosphere enveloping him lovingly, patiently, steadily week after week will prove a sheet anchor for him to tie to until he gets his bearings and will do more than anything else to help him bridge the transition from soldier to civilian.

So, then, if the reader is disappointed that this book contains few neatly packaged rules for dealing with the returned soldier, let him realize that its chief purpose is to help in bringing about an atmosphere of understanding that will prove infinitely more constructive than reliance on any set of instructions. Instructions in living are pretty futile, anyway. No two persons ever react precisely the same to similar situations, and what is good advice for one person may turn out to be the worst possible advice for another. Overcoming difficulties in adjusting to people and the world around us is one of the major necessities in the lives of us all. It is normal to have to face problems of adjustment and it is equally normal to find some of them difficult to face. In this respect the returned soldier is not different from the rest of us, except that his problems of adjustment, because of his military experiences, take on a somewhat different coloring from ours or possess a special intensity. In his struggles to adapt himself to civilian living you and I can help if we try to learn a new language; *i.e.*, the language of behavior. This is not a language of the spoken word nor of the written one. Instead, it is a language that helps us to understand *why* people act as they do through understanding the meaning (often a hidden meaning) of their behavior.

Why, for example, does one ex-soldier keep a grim-lipped silence and refuse to talk about his war experiences, while another embarrasses his family with his ceaseless loquacity on this subject? What is another trying awkwardly to tell us through his actions when he restlessly throws up one good job after another and won't settle down? What is the meaning of the behavior of a third when he soon becomes snappish toward the mother or wife he idealized while overseas? Why does the formerly self-sufficient and self-confident soldier now act fearful, timid, and unsure? What disguised cry for help is still another trying to send us when he avoids former friends and clings solely with almost a desperate tenacity to buddies and other servicemen? And why is it that yet another refuses to seek a job because he cannot be convinced that his symptoms of palpitation, shortness of breath, and tiredness on exertion do not come from "heart disease" despite the assurances of eminent specialists that his heart is sound? The various behaviors of these men are not due to sheer cussedness or perversity. They have meaning and significance. These men are trying to tell us who care for them that they feel confused, frightened, anxious, but their message is conveyed in actions rather than in the words they cannot find. It is up to us, then, if we are to be of genuine help, to fathom the meaning of these actions and make our own reactions constructive.

Should we succeed in mastering this language of behavior two results will accrue: first, we shall be enabled to view the man in whom we are interested as of a sameness with ourselves, as another human being groping in the face of difficulty to find ways of reconciling his ambitions, cravings, need for security, and his deep-seated instincts with the necessity for socially effective and acceptable living; and secondly, the atmosphere of understanding so much talked about in preceding paragraphs automatically will be created. In this event, the returned soldier no longer will seem a stranger, for we shall be able to penetrate behind his façade of "strangeness" and in having its meaning revealed to us shall see much of ourselves. This is why, should we fail to acquire facility in using this "language," it will be hurtful to him if we continue to envisage him as a strange being set apart from the rest of us by reason of his military experiences or as one to be absolved from the responsibilities of ordinary adult existence. After all, this is a people's war, and the soldier in our democracy is a cross section representative of us all. The current of our American life flows in and through him. His problems of adjustment after his military service are not mysterious or impossible to fathom, but merely variations or exaggerations of our own. We *can* put ourselves in his place and understand how he feels. We *can* create for him a climate of comprehension that will foster self-reliance and leave him free to come to grips successfully with his task. To assist us all in achieving these goals is the reason for this book.

What *are* some of the problems of adjusting back to civilian life of the returned soldier? To answer this it will help if first we try to visualize what kind of a person this man was before he became a soldier. Here are the facts. The armed forces of the United States of America in this World War II number approximately eleven million persons. Because, as stated above, this is a people's war, these eleven million have been drawn from literally all walks of life, and the army became a civilian rather than a professional army. Professional fighting was not the prewar trade of these civilians, and they knew little of it. They had entered the armed forces, some by enlistment but most by a process of enforced selective service. Some came from parents born in Naples or Prague or Copenhagen, while the parents of others came from Boston's Beacon Street. Some had been mechanics and others clerks; some had taught school while others had herded sheep on Western ranges. Some were divinity students and others gangsters. Business executives found themselves barracks mates with union organizers, and farmers from Vermont's boulder-studded fields drilled alongside city slickers from Broadway. But they had one characteristic in common: none of them knew about war or its methods.

Not only was this civilian army made up of men from different vocations, but the widest possible differences were to be found in their personalities and temperaments. Some were naturally stolid and phlegmatic, while others were equally naturally quick and excitable. Some invariably were sober and serious, while others had always been frivolous or scatterbrained. Some had learned to become responsible and reliable, while others had developed habits of irresponsibility and instability. Some grew up passively accepting authority while others passionately hated it. Some were emotionally mature, while many others, normally developed in physique and intelligence, still were children in their feelings. Some remained tied to their mothers while others had long before reached man's estate.

Moreover, the attitudes of these eleven million men varied enormously about the necessity for going to war. Some adolescents (of all physical ages and craving excitement) were fairly "rarin' to go," while some older men with family responsibilities were plunged into a conflict of loyalties between love of country on the one hand and love for children, wives, or mothers, on the other. Some men other than conscientious objectors held reasoned scruples about the wisdom of war as a solution for any national problem, while others brazenly admitted they didn't give a damn about the war; they wanted only to be left alone in their accustomed surroundings. Some welcomed entrance into the army as a means of escaping from burdensome home obligations, while a few with perhaps a criminal record behind them hastened eagerly to induction as a lesser evil than a threatened jail sentence. But eager, resentful, conflicted, or indifferent, into military life they all went to have their varying attitudes and temperaments hammered into a common pattern of military usefulness.

These are the men, or in another sense this is a composite of the man, who went to war, met a variety of strange experiences, either adjusted eventually to his new environs or failed to adjust (*i.e.*, developed a "psychiatric" handicap), and now is back home again. What is he faced with? How does he feel about it? What *are* his problems of adjustment to civilian life?

First, if he has been in the service any length of time, the problem of functioning on his own once more, unsupported by the group of which he had become a welded part; second, the problem of adjusting to the disillusionment of discovering that the folks back home are just humans after all, and not the idyllic creatures his nostalgic-ridden mind had envisioned in a foxhole in Normandy; third, his conviction that no one who had not been "over there" possibly could understand how he feels about things, with resulting loneliness, insecurity, and a sense of isolation—these are a few of the broad, general problems of adjustment the returned soldier has to face. In addition, however, there are a host of lesser, if more urgent, ones that besiege him. What to do about a job? Shall he go back to the old one or try another? If he has been discharged before the war was ended, perhaps for some psychiatric difficulty that shows no physical wounds, how shall he save his face and explain it? In that case, will he have to start fresh in some town where he was not previously known, or brazen it out with old friends by substituting some fictitious but plausible physical reason for his discharge, like flat feet or a heart condition? What will he do about the problem of realizing that his hasty war marriage was a well-meant mistake and that he and the bride he never really got to know are not suited for the long pull together? If he had been married for some years previously and his wife went to work on his departure, how will he deal with her reluctance to give up an outlet that she has come to enjoy? If she had gone back to live with her mother, will he have a time prying her loose from the in-laws? If he has become physically or psychologically disabled in part, how much will he give in to the temptation of becoming wholly dependent and being taken care of without effort on his part?

These are but a fraction of the multitudinous problems of adjustment faced not alone by the discharged soldier, but by all soldiers, sick or well, mature or immature. They are not chimerical problems but very real and some of them very painful to solve. But solved they must be, in one way or another, if lives are to be salvaged for effective living and if postwar destinies are to be realized.

Although this book deals with the adjustment problems of all returned servicemen—the demobilized of the future as well as the discharged of the present—it would fail of its purpose if it did not give special attention to some of the problems of adjustment of those men who are separated from military service because of what are called "psychiatric" reasons. Contrary to wide public opinion, the term "psychiatric" is not a synonym for "insane." In its military usage "psychiatric" usually merely designates a departure from average personality traits or temperament, or it is a label perhaps for certain attitudes, or for symptoms of functional illness, that render a soldier unsuitable for *military* service. The term "military service" purposely is stressed since a large number of men discharged from the army or navy because of psychiatric reasons were able, and will continue to be able, to function in a civilian environment. Thus, all it means as used in wartime is that by reason of some disorder of personality a given man cannot exercise those qualities that are essential in the

disability they present. In this connection it has been found that psychiatric casualties are *sixteen times* more likely to result in permanent disabilities than other kinds of illness.

If this is the situation with regard to World War I, we can glimpse at least the outline of what the situation already is threatening to become in World War II, with its nearly three times as many men involved. This is why no book on the problems of adjustment of returning servicemen can overlook the special problems of a group so huge that it constitutes almost half of all men discharged for medical reasons.

If we are to help the returned soldier in whom we are interested to deal wisely with his problems of adjustment on coming home, we should logically understand some of the things that happened to him while he was away. We should understand, for example, what military life meant to him, what it did to him, how military authorities endeavored to strengthen him against the strains of his new life, and how also they tried to lessen these strains.

It may strike readers as strange or unnecessary to go back so far in a person's former life in order to understand his present problems. But it is impossible to truly comprehend the returned serviceman as he is today and the reasons for his attitudes unless we first see clearly what kind of a person this man of ours was before he became a soldier or sailor and, most of all, what equipment he took with him to be affected for better or worse by the experiences that military life imposed on it. No two men took into the army with them exactly the same equipments of temperament, personality, and native endowment, and consequently no two of them met the experiences—even identical experiences—of military life in identically the same way. The same truism will hold good when they come home. No two ex-servicemen are going to react in precisely the same manner to the problems of adjusting to civilian life, and by a reverse process the equipments they brought out of the army with them will prove a help or a hindrance in making those adjustments. In the next chapter, therefore, we have to commence our process of understanding and helping the returned soldier to adjust to civilian life by beginning at the beginning, *i.e.*, by discussing some of the equipment with which he left home.

2

WHAT EQUIPMENT DID THE NEW SOLDIER TAKE WITH HIM?

WHEN the new soldier first reported at his training camp or his boot camp or any other kind of receiving station, he was issued some equipment. This included a uniform, perhaps a rifle and an ammunition belt, and some other purely military paraphernalia. However, long before he first reported for duty, life had issued him some other equipment. This included a healthy body and an assortment of psychological baggage. His physical equipment must have been reasonably good, otherwise he could not have passed through the rigorous screening procedures given at the time of his induction board examinations. These examinations included minute attention to his eyes, his ears, his heart, and other bodily organs, as well as to the state of his emotional life and his personality. To be sure, this screening process did not always function without mistakes. The examinations at induction centers were usually conducted by medical specialists of outstanding reputation. Nevertheless, the numbers of men to be examined were so great and the time in which to undertake the examinations was so limited (seldom more than three or four minutes for each specialist) that errors occasionally were bound to occur. Generally speaking, however, and with some inevitable exceptions, when the man in whom we are interested finally passed his induction board medical examinations and was taken into military service, he was likely to be a hand-picked person in the very literal meaning of this phrase, and throughout his entire military experience thereafter no human being on earth received more or better attention from medical officers in maintaining his physical efficiency at a high peak.

So much for the physical equipment which this man took into service with him, but what about the psychological equipment he also took with him? Psychological make-up was less conspicuous than a soundly functioning body or lean, hard muscles, but it was an equally important part of his total equipment and played an even more vital role in helping him to make adjustments to the multitudinous experiences of military life.

First among the man's psychological apparatus was his constitutional endowment. This does not mean so much the things that his heredity conferred on him, such as the brown hair of his father or the blue eyes of his mother, as it means less tangible endowments, like his personal amount of aggressiveness or passivity, his capacity to resist strains and fatigue, whether physical or mental, and the like. His intelligence, for example, is one of many qualities that go to make up this thing that we call constitutional endowment. When our man was born into the world he was given an ability to develop more or less intelligence. The amount of this ability, however, was predetermined or fixed in advance and so also, to a considerable extent, was his particular rate of intellectual development. Perhaps our man was one of those persons who naturally possess a rapid rate of intellectual development, but it is equally possible that he might be one of those others in whom this quality grows more slowly. However, if his early training and his early experiences were propitious, the chances are that by the time he reached twenty years of age he also reached his maximum growth of native intelligence. To be sure, he will continue to acquire training and experience for many years to come, which lead to greater efficiency in life and to better judgment; but it is important to understand that the original ability that helped him to profit by training and experience will not go on increasing after he reaches his maximum intellectual growth, which, as stated before, is around twenty years of age. At the various induction centers all over the country a man is acceptable for military service if his intelligence, when figured on a mental age level, is at least ten years. The chances are, of course, that it is higher than this, but as democratic institutions our army and navy utilize all grades of intelligence from border line feeble-minded at one end of the scale to college graduates and Phi Beta Kappas at the other.

Another constitutional endowment included in our man's psychological make-up is his body-mind integration: *i.e.*, his degree of balanced functioning of his nervous system and of the various organs affected by this system. This nervous system is the great coordinator. When it is in healthy running order it causes all the different parts of the body to function smoothly as a harmonious whole. Sometimes, however, when a state of imbalance exists, the individual has a less-than-average ability to resist strains and pressures such as excitement, fatigue, rapid changes in environment, etc. One of many examples that could be used to illustrate this is found in the man or woman who invariably gets carsick whenever he rides on a train or in automobiles; another is the person who on slight provocation under the influence of fear or even of such simple things as changes in environment may sweat profusely, experience palpitation of the heart, and have his face and neck flush up to an uncomfortable extent. If these things happen it may not mean that the person's stomach or heart is necessarily damaged, but merely that the function of these organs is disturbed. In other words, it represents the differences between a disease, or physical damage of an organ of the body, and a disorder of the function of that organ. Not infrequently these symptoms represent an instability of what is called the "vasomotor system." When, as a result possibly of poor constitutional endowment, an individual has an exceptionally excitable vasomotor system that is easily thrown off balance, he tends to react to various experiences in extreme degrees. The child or adult who habitually becomes delirious and goes out of his head with every trivial fever or rise in temperature may be an example of this, and we say that his physiological integration is poor or unstable.

A man's temperament is yet another aspect of his constitutional endowment. His customary tendency to be phlegmatic or excitable, to be outgoing and sociable or, oppositely, to be seclusive and withdrawn, to have swings of mood from elation to depression; to be habitually "touchy" and hypersensitive and overserious in contrast to being easygoing or scatterbrained—all these qualities and many more go to make up a person's temperament, and, while they are susceptible of being lessened or increased by the nature of the experiences the person meets in life, their real roots are believed to be embedded in his constitutional endowment, and the man in whom we are interested took *his* particular temperament into military life with him to affect his adjustment for better or worse.

Yet another article in the new soldier's psychological baggage is his particular assortment of acquired or learned habits [or "patterns"] of meeting similar situations in life in similar ways. This is a most interesting process in the lives of us all, and because it is so likely to affect our adjustment it seems worth while to discuss it a bit. Very early in life every one of us began to lay down patterns or habits of reacting to similar experiences in similar ways. During the course of an ordinary lifetime each of us meets up with thousands of experiences, but when we commence to analyze these different experiences we soon realize that, while many are superficially different, nevertheless most can be reduced to a few common denominators. It is surprising, indeed, to note how few are the really basic experiences in the life of any one of us, and most of the difficult things that happen to us can be classified under the heading of meeting frustration, or disappointment, or loss, or having to accept the imposition of authority.

These are some of the life experiences that come to everyone and they constitute our common lot in compelling us to learn how to adjust to the world around us. Even the tiny baby is not immune to the experience of being frustrated in some of his wishes or to feeling a sense of loss or to being disappointed. As he continues to meet these various basic experiences in his life, he tends to form a habit or a pattern of reacting to them. Thus, one child faced by some thwarting of his wishes begins by reacting to such an experience in terms of a temper tantrum, while a second child may react to a frustrating experience by sulking and trying to make people give in by causing them to feel sorry for him, or yet again a third reacts to disappointment or loss by withdrawing into himself and building up an inner world of fantasy and unrealistic daydreaming to compensate himself for his loss. It makes little difference what the mode of reaction is. The point of it all is that, after an individual has reacted to a certain kind of experience in a certain fashion over a long enough time, he automatically develops the habit or pattern of meeting *all* experiences of that kind during his lifetime in the same stereotyped way. As will be seen later, it is important to understand this because the habits or patterns that the soldier laid down during the developmental years of his life are going to play a considerable role in determining not only how he adjusted to military life, but more particularly how he is going to adjust to his return home when he is either discharged or demobilized. He takes these assortments of habits or patterns into military service with him as part of his psychological equipment and sometimes, if they are unhealthy, the patterns may make his adjustment painful unless they can be unlearned.

The cultural conditioning of our man is still another article of equipment he took with him. As Americans, it has long been our pride that we are a composite of many peoples, not only from many different lands but from differing regions within our own country. A boy, for example, whose parents came from Italy may have a different cultural conditioning from a boy whose parents spent their early lives in Denmark. By the same token a serviceman who spent most of his life on a farm in the South is apt to have a different cultural conditioning from another who spent all the previous years of his life in a busy city in the North. It should be made clear, of course, that we are not talking about the superiority of any one culture over another. It is merely a recognition of differences in culture, which include differences in folklore and in attitudes toward such simple things as customs in eating, amusement, friendliness to strangers, and a long list of additional items. More, even, than our public schools does military life bring men of different backgrounds closely together, and no small part of the initial adjustment to military life is that necessitated by a man who reflects one cultural background in learning to respect and adapt himself to a man from another. The indispensable close living of military life promotes tolerance, and, if a man happens to come from a home where cultural intolerance in some measure or other was prevalent, his newly won broad-mindedness may make for adjustment difficulties with the members of his own narrow family on his return.

Another piece of psychological apparatus taken into military service with a man is his backlog of civilian skills and his special vocational abilities or disabilities. To an extent never before attempted, the army and navy have endeavored to discover the special vocational abilities of the men in service and to assign them as far as may be possible to jobs that can constructively utilize such abilities. This process is highly systematized and begins at the reception center where the man first reports after acceptance by the induction board. He spends a week or more in this reception center, during which he is personally interviewed and his educational, vocational, and social history is obtained. He is also given various aptitude and other tests, and on the basis of all these he is assigned to a type of activity where his abilities can best be used. Special talents or experience are particularly sought for.

Mistakes, of course, have been made here and there, as is inevitable in dealing with as large a group as some eleven million persons. However, it is astonishing to see how a man entering military service with some special skill is encouraged to advance his knowledge of that skill during his service and to adapt it to military use. This war is particularly a war of machines, and, unlike the young men of most other nations, our American soldiers and sailors have for the most part been reared in a mechanized environment. There is an excellent chance that the man in whom we are interested entered service with at least a rudimentary familiarity with mechanical skills, which, depending both on need and on opportunity, undoubtedly were sharpened by further training in a military environment. Scores of other skills, too, have been taken by their possessors into military life to be subjected to further intensive training. Such advanced training will be of help in furnishing these men with a sense of vocational security on their return home and at this time it appears likely that vocational retraining following the demobilization period may not be needed quite so much as was the case following the close of World War I.

Last, but perhaps most important, of all the equipment taken by our man into military service is his personal degree of emotional maturity. By this is meant particularly his capacity on most occasions to "act his age" and be free to a reasonable extent from emotional dependency on parents or parent symbols. Reaching an acceptable degree of freedom from emotional dependency on parents is one of the primary tasks confronting all adolescent boys and girls, and, since the army and navy are made up of a goodly percentage of adolescents and persons in their post-adolescent stage of mental development, the attainment of emotional maturity has profound repercussions both on military life and on civilian readjustment afterward. An emotionally immature person is one who meets one of the basic experiences in life not as the average person of his own age and background ordinarily meets such an experience, but rather as a younger person would meet an experience of this kind. Reluctance or even inability to take average responsibility for oneself and the management of one's own behavior is one example of this. The need to lean or depend on another person to an excessive degree for solving trivial problems or for making minor decisions is still another. Reacting to still other life experiences in what is generally called a "childish" way is yet a third example of immaturity. Emotional immaturity has nothing to do with a person's intelligence, nor is it visible in his physical make-up. It is much more subtle than that and is to be found in the make-ups of those from the highest to the lowliest walks in life. Army officers in high command may be emotionally immature just as much as the obscure private, but whether he is in high position or low, in many ways a man's degree of emotional maturity is going to determine how satisfactory are both his military and his civilian adjustment.

The emotionally mature person can be recognized by several characteristics habitually in evidence. Dr. Maurice Levine, a psychiatrist in Cincinnati, describes some of these in a chapter of his book *Psychotherapy in Medical Practice*.[1]

[1] Published by The Macmillan Company, New York.

"One characteristic of the emotionally mature person is his ability to live his life to a greater degree in terms of the actual realities that confront him, rather than in terms of his wishes, his phantasies, or his fears. Children to a great extent live in terms of their wishes and fears. A lonely child may deny the reality of his loneliness by pretending that he has playmates, and live in a phantasy world. In childhood play this is good fun; in the serious aspects of adult life, it means that one is tricking oneself and seeing things crookedly. . . . Another characteristic of emotional maturity is the tendency to live one's life in terms of long-time values rather than in short-time values. As human beings grow older, as they have to make an adjustment to other people they have to learn to give up momentary pleasures for the sake of more lasting ones; they have to become willing to defer immediate satisfactions when those satisfactions would block or stultify or destroy the more lasting satisfactions in life. One of the best criteria of maturity is the capacity to stand a necessary, temporary frustration. . . .

"Yet another characteristic of emotional maturity is the ability to be independent. This does not mean the blustering defiance of authority in the guise of 'independence,' nor an unwillingness to take advice, that may be camouflaged under the need to be self-sufficient. This does not mean the sort of independence that masks the desire to be the dominant one in a situation, or that conceals the urge to run other people's lives, to play the 'big boss.' It does mean, however, an independence of this kind; that the individual is able to stand on his own feet when necessary, that he is not still tied to his parents' apron strings, that he is not constantly dependent upon others for advice in trivial situations, that he is able to take some reasonable responsibility for himself, and that he does not have an excessive amiability or willingness to give in. . . . The capacity to have a reasonable dependence on others is still a third characteristic of the emotionally mature person. Inter-personal relationships involve an inter-dependence. Cooperation involves being on the receiving end as well as the giving end, in work, in marriages, in play, and in friendships. The ability to take advice when it is pertinent and contributory to one's own decision and responsibility, the capacity to be able to receive love and friendship from others, to be able to accept when others want to give; these are mature and valid characteristics. Some people are unable to receive or to be wholesomely dependent because their pride is hurt if they are not the giver; to them, giving means strength and power, while receiving means playing second fiddle, being inferior. A mature person can give a great deal, but he can also enjoy receiving."

This need to be reasonably mature in the development of one's feelings or emotional life is of the utmost importance when it comes to making an adjustment, first of all to military life and subsequently to the man's return home in the community. This may be clearer if we look for a moment at the processes through which a person goes before he reaches normal emotional adulthood or emotional maturity. The process starts in early infancy when, very properly and very necessarily, the little child is completely dependent upon his parents for everything; his food, his shelter, his protection, and even his very thoughts and ideas. As he grows up, however, the little child begins to do some thinking for himself, and he finds, sometimes to his consternation, that his thoughts about certain matters do not any longer always agree with those of his parents. Sometimes this creates in him a feeling of guilt as if somehow he were disloyal to his parents, but at the same time his independence of thinking continues, driven, as it were, by an almost biologic urge. As he grows older and enters upon the stage of adolescence this inner urge for independence becomes greater and its outward expression often is found in that type of behavior sometimes labeled "adolescent rebellion." During this adolescent period the boy or girl is apt to be conflicted and torn between opposing wishes. One part of him wishes to grow up and become independent and to learn how to stand on his own feet, in other words, to become a real adult. The other part of him, however, remembers with nostalgia the protected, carefree, happy-go-lucky days of childhood, when no responsibility was thrust upon him and when he was sheltered not only in a physical sense but also in a psychological sense. Out of this conflict emerge various types of adolescent behavior, which may affect the individual's subsequent life adjustment. Nevertheless, if the adolescent has had wise parents and if luck has been with him eventually he muddles through to an adjustment to life satisfactorily enough to justify the designation "mature."

On the other hand, a number of children during their developmental years have had obstacles thrown in their path toward eventual emancipation from dependence on parents and parental symbols. Sometimes these obstacles are found in the attitudes of the parents themselves, who unwittingly are reluctant to have their children grow up and leave them or become freed from their control and who tend, therefore, to make the protected era of childhood so attractive that the youngster finds little incentive to leave it. On occasions other types of obstacles, over which not even parents have control, serve to prolong the normal period of dependency so that, while the boy or girl is growing up physically and intellectually in proper fashion, his emotional growth—in some respects at least—remains retarded.

The economic depression through which this country passed a decade ago is one example of this. The effects of this depression on the journey toward maturity of hundreds of thousands of our young people are likely to be seen in the ways these persons will make their postwar adjustments. During those ten terrible years of national depression, unemployment and privation stalked the land and only a program of vast public relief could be depended upon for the bare necessities of existence for millions of families. As a consequence tens of thousands of our men in military service today spent the most formative and susceptible years of their lives in an emotional atmosphere tempered by a temptation toward dependency. During those lean years untold numbers of these then children could never remember a steadily employed father or a time when the family life did not center around the weekly food basket or the check from the Relief Bureau. Equally many of these adolescents never had an opportunity to work for themselves for wages, and legions of them extended high-school or college courses as substitutes for jobs that were not to be had. Under the circumstances large numbers of them began imperceptibly to endow the Relief Bureau—and more remotely the "Government"—with parental qualities of support and assumption of responsibility. This, of course, was no fault of theirs or of their parents, and for many it was unavoidable. Nevertheless, as a consequence the journey toward adult maturity and independence of countless thousands of young people slowed down under the necessity for yielding some of the freedom they were just beginning to win in favor of a return to enforced dependency. What is said here implies no criticism of the purposes or programs of Relief. There are many, including this writer, who are convinced that our nation could not have survived those disastrous years without Relief. However, recognition of its need and appreciation of its value cannot obscure the fact that, while Relief went far to solve one national problem, its implicit, if unavoidable, invitation to dependency created another of even more enduring complexity.

Thus it happens that a substantial number of the men in military service today are the products of this depression and dependency era. The temptation to return, emotionally speaking, to an earlier stage of development in which they were taken care of has been embedded deeply in their make-up. Not all, of course, will yield to this temptation when they leave military service, but some will, and the numbers of these doubtless will be large enough to create a national problem of much consequence when it comes to assuming once more the responsibilities of independent living after the war. The precise details of the national problem that may well be precipitated by these emotionally immature and dependency-conditioned individuals are not yet clear, but the general shape of the problem is discernible and will almost certainly include demands by this group of ex-servicemen not only for pensions, but, in the case of many, for indefinitely prolonged hospitalization of mental and physical conditions for which excessive institutionalization is the worst possible treatment, if the assumption of self-support and independent living is the goal of treatment.

One of the most vulnerable bits of psychological baggage taken into military service by the man in whom we are interested consists therefore of his personal degree of emotional maturity (which includes his relative freedom from emotional dependency). If he happened to be in the stage of adolescence when he went into service he was probably engaged unconsciously in bursting his final shackles of childhood dependency on his parents, and what happened to him after entering military service might well have tipped the balance, in the direction either of proceeding to emancipation or, on the other hand, of regressing to a more dependent state of existence.

War, with its military need for obedience to orders and its frequent subordination of individuality, independent thinking, and self-direction, offers scant incentive to adolescents who need for their own salvation to complete their emancipation from childhood dependency on parental symbols. It is not, of course, a predestined certainty that all soldiers on their return to the community will yield to this "call of the cradle," but the temptation at least will be there, and we who receive these men back to our bosoms can do much to keep the temptation from becoming a reality by making adulthood more attractive than eternal childhood.

These, then, are some of the articles of hidden equipment that every soldier takes into war with him. That they cannot be seen with the eyes or touched with the fingers does not lessen their importance as tools that make military adjustment easy or difficult. If among this psychological baggage

SOLDIER TO CIVILIAN

there be articles of maturity, outgoingness, and resiliency of personality, the recent civilian finds his adjustment to the new life not too arduous. On the other hand, if it contains an oversupply of rigidity, fragile personality traits, or eccentricity, then trouble in adaptation of one kind or another is bound to ensue. It is important to realize, however, that no matter what kind of psychological equipment was taken into military service by the man in whom we are interested, the new life did things to that equipment, and the next chapter will explain the nature of some of those things.

3

WHAT DID MILITARY SERVICE DO
TO THE FORMER CIVILIAN?

FROM the day that a man reported at the induction station military service began to do things to him. Some of these things were to his advantage and others perhaps were not, but, healthy or unhealthy, the new life hurled demand after demand on him for adjustment to a bewildering set of changes. Among these adjustments three stand out with particular prominence: (1) adjustment to the loss of individuality; (2) adjustment to separation from entrenched habits of living and from accustomed interpersonal relationships; (3) adjustment to the loss of the freedom he possessed in civilian life to shape his surroundings and environment in accordance with his own needs or wishes.

Of all human possessions our individuality or our awareness of self as a special sort of person is the most prized. Lessen our sense of personal identity and you throw open the door to lowered self-esteem and make easy the entrance of feelings of inferiority and anxiety. In civilian life the most mousy of us will fight to the last ditch to maintain some individuality, that need to make the world aware of us as different—even in a slight way—from the mass of others. But military life necessarily exerts strong discouragement to individuality. War is a group experience, especially modern war, and there is scant place in it for the retention of centrifugally directed traits or mannerisms. In battle the safety of the group often depends on the action of the group as a whole, not on any one individual, and more than one combat catastrophe has been reported as due to the insistence of one person to break away from concerted group action. This is why military authorities deliberately inculcate the submergence of self from the very day the soldier or sailor reports for duty.

The lengths to which this necessary process goes prove disturbing at first to many men, especially those who in civilian life had become accustomed to emphasizing their individualities, such as professional men, artists, and the like. Disturbing or not, all men in military service are subjected to some degree of that process someone has termed the "attainment of anonymity." Two army psychiatrists, Drs. Maskin and Altman,[1] describe this process vividly:

"The very uniform the soldier wears obscures identity, and his personal name is replaced by a serial number. Anonymity is enhanced by distinction-obliterating activities, such as constant waiting in line, marching in cadence, mass calisthenics. The individual loses significance in his own right and merges imperceptibly into the background of platoon or company. . . . The soldier can rarely be alone. He sleeps in a barracks and uses an open latrine.

[1] "Psychological Factors in the Transition from Civilian to Soldier," *Psychiatry*, Vol. 6, No. 3.

There are no situations where his privacy cannot be invaded. The initiative for personality functioning passes into other hands. The soldier starts and stops at commands; his activities are predetermined by regulation. . . . It is no longer as in civilian life, 'What do I think, feel, want?'—but—'What is the directive?'—Familiar old functions of self-planning are denied."

Loss of individuality of this kind is but one of the things that going into military service does to a man. In time, however, he comes to accept it and grow used to it. Indeed, except for a few whose need to cling to individuality was so deeply rooted that even military life could not dent it (and these sometimes acquired labels as "disciplinary problems" or "misfits"), he probably came to depend and lean on this submergence of self, at least to a degree. A man found, rather to his surprise, that he derived a sort of group support from the experience; if it was necessary to efface the former self, then by compensation he began to discover a new self—a Company X self, a Division Y self, a Battleship Z self. From a military point of view this growth of identification with the group is highly desirable and is encouraged at every point. And so long as our man remained in military service he likely found it a source of security. In it he found two, at least, of the chief ingredients that go into the making of a feeling of security (*i.e.*, emotional security)—a realization of "belongingness" and a realization of acceptance. Even in everyday life we must discover these ingredients if we are to become reasonably secure in our feelings and in our relationships to others. We must come to realize for example, that we "belong" to the group of which we are a part. This means realization of belongingness to our family group, our school group, and our shop or office or work group and, if we are to attain to true emotional maturity, the realization that we belong to the rest of mankind.

It is not enough, however, to feel that we "belong" if we are to be emotionally secure. In addition we must achieve a realization that the others in whatever group we have attained belongingness accept us as one of that group. Thus, it is insufficient to realize that we belong to the Smith or the Jones family, or the A factory, or the B office, or the C church. Beyond all this if we are to feel really secure we must realize as well, that the others in the family or the factory or the office or the church *accept* us as one of themselves. "In union there is strength" is a trite enough adage, but nowhere is it truer than in personal relationships.

If a new soldier must adjust to loss of his individuality when he goes into the service, it is not all loss, therefore, but some gain through group identification, at least while he is in active service. Once he returns to civilian life, however, the story is apt to be reversed, and in a later chapter mention will be made of how the relinquishment of his hard-won security through identification with the group makes his home adjustment difficult, when once more he finds himself on his own.

Men with certain personality characteristics or backgrounds of life experiences fit more easily into this need for loss of individuality than others. For example, the chronically shy, self-effacing person may welcome the anonymous existence of army or navy life as a sort of refuge and take to it with avidity. Likewise, the passive, dependent personality with scant self-initiative or self-motivation may find comfortable the military environment that takes over for him the need for making decisions or for assuming responsibilities that might bring him to attention through "sticking his neck out" as an assertive individual. On the other hand, some professional men as discussed previously; some men with strong exhibitionistic or narcissistic qualities; or others with outstanding racial or regional characteristics that they may have found it expedient to capitalize in civilian life, find the army's demand for submergence of these traits a sore trial.

Pfc. David Evans of an infantry company offers a good example of the trials and tribulations encountered by some men in adjusting to loss of individuality. Private Evans stood out in his company like a sore thumb. He was intelligent enough—indeed, his embittered sergeant often thought too much so for his own good—but he seemed to have a constitutional aversion to doing things the way his buddies did. If army regulations prescribed wearing fatigue caps tilted over the right eye, Private Evans was always "forgetting" and would wear his over the left, and if blankets on barracks cots were supposed to be folded back a precise four inches Private Evans thought it looked better if he set his at five.

Moreover, he was invariably finding new or different ways of performing duties. On maneuvers when his platoon agreed to try to ambush an enemy column from woods at the right, Evans would be found, like as not, slithering off in response to some improved ideas of his own through open fields on the left. If the grenade instructor demonstrated how to lob them with an overhand swing, this individualist was sure his underhand throw was more effective.

It wasn't that he wanted to be insubordinate. He just naturally had to do things *his* way. Often enough, his way proved in the end to be an improvement, but it as frequently interfered with unanimous group action when group unity might mean the very lives of his comrades.

How did Private Evans get that way? The answer is simple. He merely carried over into his military life the same habits of individualism that had characterized him as a civilian. He tried conscientiously to fit himself into the military pattern of a team worker and to sink his individuality into the common picture. But it was no go.

Even as a youngster Dave Evans was a trial to his teachers and his parents. If his boyhood crowd wanted to swim in the pool below the dam Dave argued brilliantly on the advantages of the river. If it was the vogue of the moment for boys to wear crew cuts Dave remained conspicuous for his long, unbarbered hair. If airplane modeling chanced to be the accepted recreation for the majority, then young Evans would be found diligently absorbed in model railroads. Later, in his first year at college, when most of his classmates were going into fraternities, Dave declined invitation after invitation and stood out as an independent.

Private Evans finally was wounded and discharged to his home, and there were dark mutterings among some of his company that he was lucky not to have been court-martialed. At Saipan, Private Evans and three companions were sent out on a reconnaissance task. Their instructions were that if they were cut off by the enemy they were to take shelter, remain silent, and wait until a rescuing party came for them. The group was cut off, they did take shelter, and for a time they did keep silence.

But after some seven hours of this Private Evans thought up one of his better ideas. His companions expostulated vigorously in whispers but Evans's reasoning was so clever and apparently unassailable that they gave in against their better judgments. Evans's idea was to wriggle off a way, and then fire at the enemy to divert attention while the others made a dash for safety. He didn't know that at that very moment a rescuing party was approaching silently, hoping to take the Japs by surprise. And so Private Evans as per his plan did send a burst of shots against the little brown men, whereupon bedlam broke loose. The position of the rescuing party was disclosed and for a few moments it was nip and tuck whether they would all be wiped out. Happily, they managed to get away, but with several wounded, of whom Private Evans was one. His individuality just could not be submerged in the interests of the group to a point where he was safe to have around, and his buddies heaved sighs of relief when he was evacuated.

The second of our three major demands for adjustment on going into military life is for adaptation to the loss of familiar or deeply entrenched habits of living and to separation from accustomed inter-personal relationships.

A considerable number of men leaving home for military service welcomed this separation. A few, of course, frankly used compulsory military service as a socially acceptable excuse for deserting their families without having to suffer the customary penalties of legal action or of gnawing conscience. Many others, however, plodding faithfully with family responsibilities nevertheless yearned secretly for a "vacation" from them. They would rather be torn apart by wild horses than publicly admit such a yearning, but in their inner hearts they welcomed the temporary relief conferred by military service from family control, responsibility, and obligations. The married man of this kind was likely to have anticipated his army experience as a sort of return to bachelor freedom, and he gladly yielded up to his wife (with, perhaps, a display of face-saving reluctance) the irksome details of family management—complete control over the children, payment of taxes, mortgage installments, renewal of automobile licenses, and all the other myriad irritations implied in the assumption of family responsibility. This willingness to permit his family to revert for a time to a matriarchal institution did not indicate that he was necessarily a weakling or a coward. The chances were greatly in favor of his being an averagely mature, responsible individual, who, nevertheless, objected only conventionally to Uncle Sam's invitation to shed his mantle as a "family man" and once more become "one of the boys."

And it must be admitted that, in her secret heart, more than one wife likewise welcomed—although her feelings about it may have been a bit mixed—the opportunity of becoming the actual head of the family. She may have believed (and she may have been correct in her belief) that she could manage these myriad family responsibilities more efficiently than her husband, with the result that the latter's secret sigh of relief at going off to camp was echoed by one of her own. No sooner had the front door closed on his departing figure than she, drying her tears, may have bustled into the living room to rearrange the furniture the way she had always wanted to, banished to the attic the shabby and disgraceful easy chair her husband stubbornly clung to, and instituted a new regime of disciplining the children without fear of paternal interference. Of course, like many other things in this world the shift to a matriarchal family life for the "duration" brought difficulties in its train, but those difficulties in numerous instances proved less uncomfortable than the readjustment to a patriarchal status when the husband and father returned. Some wives, given a taste of freedom, power, and total responsibility, are reluctant to relinquish these, and in a later chapter of this book will be found a discussion of the problems ensuing when Father returns to step back into his former role.

A good many unmarried men also welcomed the separation from accustomed inter-personal relationships enforced by induction into the service. Among these were a proportion of rebellious adolescents straining at the bit of parental control. They, too, yearned secretly (and some weren't at all secret about it) for a socially acceptable excuse that would make it possible to get out from under what they considered —rightly or wrongly—to be parental domination. They were under the delusion, poor kids, that once away from home and in the army they could be their own boss; no more mother around to tell them when to change a shirt; no more father to say they couldn't have the car tonight. That much of this illusion of freedom proved to be illusion came quickly to be true, but for this group of new soldiers the loss of familiar habits of living and the separation from accustomed interpersonal relationships were welcomed at the outset with enthusiasm.

For the majority of men, however, who left home to enter military service adjustment to this loss and this separation proved painful. After all, not many people really like to change their major ways of living or to have to create an entirely new set of relationships to others. To be sure, most of us in the course of a lifetime do have to make such changes, but few really welcome them. We are all essentially creatures of habit by the time we reach adult years, and monumental changes in habits are to be shunned if possible. Resilient, outgoing personalities meet these demands for changes with a bit of grousing perhaps, but they make a virtue of necessity and eventually come through all right. Rigid, negativistic personalities resist change with sometimes an astonishing tenacity, and it is among this group, along with others who are immature, dependent, or insecure, that adjustment to the loss of civilian habits and relationship securities is made with especial difficulty. Reports from army and navy training centers indicate that it is this group who contribute an appreciable percentage to those who never are able to adjust themselves to military life and who are required (unconsciously, of course) to develop emotional or physical symptoms as an outward expression of the adjustment strain they are unable to digest. In this respect it is interesting to note that the experience of military doctors indicates that of all the men who "break down" with emotional disabilities while in training camps, almost half of them "break" during the *first month* of military service; about 75 per cent experience their breakdowns within the first two months, and some 97 per cent break within six months after they begin military duty. Of course, others develop psychiatric disabilities while overseas under combat conditions, but for the most part this latter group constitutes another story to be dealt with later in this book.

One soldier of this immature kind, unable to adapt to change, became morbidly depressed and attempted suicide six weeks after reporting to a boot camp in the navy. He had made a conscientious effort to adapt himself to his new life, but the separation from his mother, his high-school gang in the small town where he had lived, and the familiar surroundings that gave him security so long as he remained tightly anchored to them proved too much. Although a splendid physical specimen, he never had grown up in his feelings and represented one of those emotionally immature personalities referred to in the preceding chapter. He was an only child whose mother unwisely clung to him for her own emotional needs and created a pathologic dependency on her. He had never been allowed to be away from home before, even for a night, and thus had never been able to achieve any degree of reliance on himself. Depression and attempted suicide, therefore, seemed to him the only way out of a situation with which he was unprepared to cope.

Another basically similar example was found in an unmarried man of thirty-five who, too, couldn't adapt himself to separation from the narrow (but protecting) circle of humdrum daily activities or from his emotional attachment to his mother. He expressed his inability to adjust to military life by becoming alcoholic and finally going A.W.O.L. Although he lived in a large city he never came to know much of it except for the immediate neighborhood in which he was born and brought up. His friendships literally were all among a small group of persons with whom he had gone to school, and his recreational interests were what many would term "narrow." He had reduced life to a formula: get up in the morning, go to the factory where he got his first job after leaving school and where he was still engaged eighteen years later on the same type of work, come home to the supper his doting mother prepared for him, read the evening paper, visit the poolrooms where his never-changing cronies hung out, return home, and go to bed. This routine seldom changed in all his years. He had never married, had few women friends, and gradually had grooved a rut in life for himself which he found comfortable. The jolt from this rut proved too much for this man, and since never before had he experienced drastic change his unpreparedness for it and his lack of ordinary resiliency made escape imperative. His method of escape was alcohol until one day, when under its influence, he gave up trying any more and extended a week-end pass from camp into a flight to home and mother. Psychiatrists at induction centers have come to learn that middle-aged personalities like the one possessed by this man—immature, unmarried, dependent (in an emotional sense) on their mothers, and living a narrow almost vegetative existence— are apt to be poor risks in the army or navy and often are rejected for military service. Incidentally, the psychiatrists have come to learn also how often such personalities become addicted to the excessive use of alcohol.

The nature of the third demand that military service makes for adjustment is another coming under the category of "loss." This particular demand has to do with the man's loss of his former freedom and ability to shape his surroundings in accordance with his desires or needs. When one stops to think about it, it is amazing how each of us living under a democracy has utilized our freedom to change our surroundings or our relationships to other people as we please. Indeed, it is this very freedom that enables many of us to get along day by day in our communities without revealing our particular quirks or eccentricities or unusual notions. Few of us are without some of these peculiarities of temperament or notions about things. If we do not happen to like outdoor work, we are free to get a job indoors; if living in close quarters with a number of people makes us uncomfortable, there are no rules against finding a room or a job where we can be semi-isolated; if we develop a prejudice against redheaded persons, we can contrive to keep away from them; if we do not like our boss at the shop or the office, we are free to quit and get a job under a more congenial supervisor; if we dislike monotony and routine, no one prevents us from seeking excitement; or if we do not happen to like change, we can always settle down in a comfortable rut of sameness.

Thus, this freedom to shape our physical and mental environments keeps many of us on a sufficiently even keel so that our little eccentricities pass unnoticed and we are not subjected to the strain of having to try to adjust to strain-provoking experiences. Once a man was in the army or navy, however, he largely lost this freedom. In military life a man found himself in a highly inelastic environment where every variation in his temperament stood out in bold relief, and, to make matters worse, he was helpless to change his environment. If being herded in with many others made him jittery and anxious in civilian life, if the requirement of living in crowded barracks or between decks in a ship accentuated these feelings, there was no way for him to do anything about lessening the strain. If he didn't like his sergeant, he couldn't quit as he would have done in the factory back home. If he didn't like change, there was no way he could prevent being transferred from unit to unit and place to place.

Many men reminiscing about their first weeks in service recall this loss of freedom as the most difficult adjustment of all. Small wonder, then, if its demands proved too great for some, although the majority muddled through eventually to an acceptable adaptation. Among those who couldn't adjust were to be found a proportion of rigid, self-centered individuals, including many whose prewar personalities were characterized by inner anxiety or fear expressed outwardly by habitual rebelliousness, or obstinacy, or perhaps negativism. Still others among this group who could not adjust to loss of the freedom to shape their environments were persons who were neurotically sick before they joined the service, persons with deep-seated mental conflicts whose ability to keep going in their civilian surroundings was so precariously balanced that changes in their daily habits or environment threw them off balance and into confusion.

Seaman Third Class Luigi Santozzi was discharged from a navy hospital after nine months of service because of "psychoneurosis." He had been acting strangely for some time, appearing depressed, tense, and anxious, but it was his numerous peculiarities that really brought him to attention. He wouldn't go to the mess hall for his meals with the others and subsisted largely on articles he purchased at the ship's canteen. He said that navy food didn't agree with him and that there were only certain things he could eat that wouldn't upset his stomach. He complained that the wool in his dark blue uniforms made him feel "queer," and once he narrowly escaped being placed in the brig for refusal to wear them. When he was required to be below decks in a shut-in place he grew panicky and once rushed about aimlessly and screaming in terror. At inspections when he had to stand at attention he squirmed and fidgeted, and more than once he was overheard muttering to himself at a sharp command from an officer.

Seaman Santozzi had been suffering from a type of neurosis for several years prior to induction into the navy, but neither he nor anyone else had ever thought of his numerous quirks and peculiarities as indicating any disorder of his emotional balance, and somehow he slipped through the induction examination without their being detected. Back in his home town Santozzi had managed by one device or another to keep his eccentricities from becoming too noticeable or too crippling.

Since childhood he had had food fads and took an inordinate interest in experimenting with various diets and their effects on his stomach and his state of chronic constipation. He drove his mother frantic with his demands for special cooking, and when at last she rebelled he would seek out vegetarian or other specialized restaurants. After a time one such restaurant would pall, but since he lived in a fair-sized city he could always hunt up another.

Then, too, he was always changing jobs. Work in those days was plentiful, and whenever he grew dissatisfied (which was often) with the nature of the work in one factory, or with the attitude of the foreman, or with his surroundings, or with the personality of the fellow who worked next to him, he would impulsively quit and soon be taken on in another. By means of these frequent changes he could contrive to keep one jump ahead of his peculiarities since he seldom remained long enough in any one place for them to become conspicuous.

He had other eccentricities, too. He developed some ideas about wool as an article of clothing. It wasn't that he was physically allergic to wool, or that it made him break out in a rash or anything. It was merely that he had ideas that somehow wool was unhealthy, and even in the cold weather he went to great pains to buy suits of clothing that contained none of this obnoxious material.

He was likewise somewhat peculiar regarding encounters with authority or with people who hurt his feelings, which, incidentally, were forever being hurt. If a foreman at the factory spoke brusquely to him Santozzi would settle the matter by quitting his job, or if a waitress failed to accord him the attention he felt was his due he would leave his meal unfinished and hunt up another place to eat.

All in all, Seaman Santozzi was a pretty sick personality, but so long as he was free to manage his life just as he pleased he could keep functioning after a fashion and avoid too many frustrations to his peculiar ideas. Once in a regimented environment like the navy, however, this freedom largely was lost. As a result Seaman Santozzi's capacity to adjust to frustrations was put to a more severe test than his neurosis would permit him to digest, and tension, anxiety, and depression were the outward manifestations of his inward inability to shape his environment any longer in accordance with his sickened ideas. Seaman Santozzi was not insane, but he was neurotically sick. This sickness made him a military liability, but back again in his community,

where he could recapture his freedom to mold his surroundings to the demands of his eccentricities, he might
go on for years without a final breakdown.

The results of the impact of military experiences on a man
in service depended then, to some extent at least, on the kind
of prewar personality that particular man had developed. As
stated in a preceding chapter, they depended on what psychological equipment the man took into service with him. While
many men were subjected to identically the same kinds of
experiences in military life, no two of them ever reacted to
those experiences in precisely the same way. For example, one
man under the unpredictable fortunes of war may have received an assignment to a station close to his home, where
for the entire duration he could visit frequently and, with
only slight changes, carry on his life pretty much as he did
in peacetimes. If he possessed one set of personality characteristics, marked, say, by immaturity, dependency, and need
to cling childishly to family protection, he may have reveled
in his good luck and performed his military duties in a satisfactory fashion. He was apt to be cheerful, happy-go-lucky,
and efficient just so long as his sheltered environment lasted.
A second man, however, in the same type of assignment but
with a different set of personality characteristics may have
chafed under the restrictions that kept him still semi-tied to
his family and grown discontented. For a dozen different reasons he may have wanted change, excitement, action, and he
resented the obligations that the accident of assignment to a
post close to home imposed on him for maintaining an existence that was neither wholly military nor wholly civilian, but
filled with the disadvantages of each.

There is humdrum routine in the army as well as in civilian life. Some thrive on it while others grow fretful. Many a man fights the entire war assigned as a hospital corpsman, spending his whole time on duty doing literally nothing but taking temperatures, or monotonously writing interminable records, or carrying bedpans in a ward. Still other uncounted thousands continue their civilian skills as bakers, butchers, cobblers, barbers, etc., in training camps and other homeland posts for the whole duration of the war. If the personalities of these men are adapted to humdrum routine, all goes well, but let them possess make-ups that in previous years caused them habitually to be restless and rarin' to go, and you are likely to have on your hands, as a reaction, a problem either of insubordination or of neurotically-determined illness.

The impact of military experiences crashes most heavily on those who eventually find themselves in combat. All the humdrum routine of the training camp now has vanished. This is the real thing, and, like all human beings, the man in whom we are interested tends to react to combat experience in terms of the kind of personality patterns (or habits) he had spent the earlier years of his life in developing. All the basic experiences of life—fear, frustration, disappointment, loss of security, reacting to authority—are now encountered in all their primitive naked strength. They have to be met, and, if humanly possible, they have to be reacted to constructively: i.e., constructively both for the man himself and for the group of which he is a part. Combat experience brings out every last personality trait of major importance that a man owns. If his entrenched patterns or habits of meeting these basic experiences have been sound in the past, the chances are that these patterns will not desert him now—with one exception to be commented on shortly. Frustration in the face of enemy fire of the wish to live, disappointment at failing to achieve at once an immediate military objective, loss of security conferred by the group when separated from companions while isolated in a foxhole, the necessity for obeying orders when these conflict with his own opinions—these are but microscopic fragments of the numerous situations in which the basic experiences of life are encountered under combat conditions.

But fragmentary as these examples are, experiences like these have to be met and reacted to, and it is now that the habitual patterns or habits a man has formed in the past will prove either a help or a hindrance in adjusting to them.

The exception referred to above is a battle experience so intense, so horrible, so ghoulish that no human being can adjust to it. Reports from military officials indicate that there are many of these, especially in this war. Under such circumstances the soundest set of personality patterns will crumble and give way to primitive fear. The resulting reactions often are labeled "psychiatric," but in view of the condition under which they are elicited they might better be labeled "natural." Lt. Col. Roy R. Grinker, a psychiatrist with the Army Air Forces, tells of one such case:

. . . a twenty-year-old platoon sergeant had been well-adjusted in civilian life with no evidences of undue anxiety, nor none in the six major engagements prior to the battle in which he came under hospital care. His platoon had orders to take a hill and had been told they would meet with no enemy opposition. The opposite proved to be true, and most of his men were wiped out by enemy machine gun fire. The patient and a friend wandered about trying to get back to their own lines, when they were caught in their own artillery fire. They finally made their way to a foxhole, where they found a dead German and an American soldier, the latter a member of their own company. The patient's friend threw the bodies out, and got into the foxhole. Shells were falling all around them and there was no room in the foxhole for the patient. He then developed intense anxiety and did not know what to do; finally he lay prone on the ground and flung the dead bodies of the two soldiers over his own for protection. He lay there for a long time, trembling and terror-stricken, until finally a shell exploded very close by and blew the two bodies off the patient, ripping off his shirt at the same time. The two dead soldiers had actually saved his life. At this point his mind went blank. He wandered about, and was picked up by some men from his company who brought him back.— When he entered one of the forward hospitals he had acute anxiety, a persistent tremor, great restlessness, loss of appetite and sleeplessness with battle dreams, in which he re-lived his battle experiences, and also had nightmares in which he saw himself being attacked by gorillas.

Colonel Grinker tells that under psychiatric care and treatment this man made an excellent recovery, his anxiety symptoms disappeared, and later he was returned to duty.

It is experiences like this that break down the most powerful adjustment capacity, and no set of personality patterns could stand up under the frightful impact of such happenings. The development—temporarily at least—of some of those myriad symptoms of "anxiety" (using this term in its technical meaning) that in the last war were called "shell shock" is the most natural thing in the world in instances like this and should never be interpreted as signs of weakness or fragility of the man's personality structure.

The question often is asked, "Will military service do something to a soldier to make a 'man' out of one who, in civilian life, had failed to reach man's estate?" Unhappily, there seem to be many well-meaning but uninformed people who believe the answer invariably is "yes." Such an answer, however, does not always fit into the facts. To be sure, more than one emotionally immature, dependent boy still tied to his mother's apron strings may have reached such a belated stage of emancipation prior to induction that all he needed was some encouragement and a final push in order to burgeon into maturity. Inducted into the army or navy, forcibly expelled from the home nest, given an opportunity under auspicious circumstances to try out his independent, fledgling wings, he may be supplied with just the push he needed to "make a man" of him. In certain other cases (but not too often), another may have had a record of civilian delinquency or police-court appearances and had reached a stage in his inner life when he was about ready to settle down, resolve the inner conflicts that caused such behavior, and turn over a new leaf. Induction into military service just at this critical time, with its opportunity for new companions, new surroundings and the enforced supervision of army or navy regulations, may furnish such a person with just the stimulus and support he requires to convert himself into an acceptable soldier.

By and large, however, the overwhelming experience of military authorities goes to show that conversion from civilian to military life does not and cannot "make a man" out of previously flaccid or distorted material. This is particularly true of a special kind of individual known as a "psychopathic personality," about which more will be explained in the next chapter. Judges, despairing parents, disillusioned wives, even some draft-board officials themselves sometimes think of the armed forces as a combination panacea and heaven-sent opportunity to get troublesome boys and men away from the community. They rationalize their motives by the pious verbalization that the new life with its rigorous discipline will "make a man" out of the troublemaker. What they are reluctant to see, however, are the real motives frequently hidden behind their rationalization. These are apt to be the human tendency to rid ourselves of discomfort by unloading the cause of it onto someone else, as well as the equally human desire to punish the person who makes us uncomfortable by advocating something unpleasant that will be good for his soul. Draft-board records are replete with requests and even demands from wives who secretly beseech that alcoholic husbands be taken into military service; from criminal court judges who are willing to make a deal with an habitual offender to suspend sentence if only the army or navy will take him; from parents of irresponsible, immature adolescents embroiled in one scrape after another, who beg the authorities to induct their offspring before he gets into the reformatory.

Understandable as these demands may be, nevertheless they are not good for the military services. Their makers need to be reminded of the trite fact that there is a war on and that you can't remake a distorted personality without spending much time in first uprooting the basic causes for the distortion. Under the urgencies of war, military officials simply do not have the time or the personnel to undertake the long-drawn-out process of refashioning the behavior patterns of men whose civilian adjustment had become habitually difficult. This is why psychiatrists on duty at the various induction stations throughout the country rigorously try to screen out and reject such inductees. Included among them are a motley group. There are those, on the one hand, for example, whose maladjustment in life is given the label of antisocial: chronic offenders, gamblers, alcoholics, drug addicts, and the like. On the other hand are included persons whose maladjustment bears the label of neurotic illness: men with compulsive behavior or obsessional thoughts, those with innumerable aches and pains without discoverable physical causation, others with stomach ulcers produced by chronic tension and anxiety. Still a third label of maladjustment includes those with personality or character difficulties such as habitual irresponsibility, unreliability, immaturity, callousness, egocentricity, or temperaments so fundamentally cool and diffident that they cannot relate themselves with average warmth to other human beings.

These are but few of the types of persons whom neither army nor navy can "make a man" of, and the services are better off without them. Some, of course, inadvertently do get into the armed forces, where most do badly. They carry over their civilian maladjustments into the military environment and become responsible for a respectable percentage of the disciplinary problems or the overfrequent hospitalization with which harried and time-pressed officials are required to cope. On returning to civilian life after discharge or demobilization these men tend to continue the same behavior patterns without having been able to profit from their military experience. No, the impact of military service seldom "makes a man" out of one who wasn't a "man" before he was inducted; the immature are likely to stay immature, the antisocial tend to remain antisocial, and the neurotically sick are seldom made well.

Not all of the things that going into military service did to a man were destructive. Life in army or navy also had its compensations, and despite the incessant but healthy "griping" that is indelibly associated with all military life unnumbered thousands of men are inwardly loathe to leave it. For one thing, they found refuge and escape in the army from myriad civilian worries, and escape, moreover, that was socially acceptable. The man who in his civilian world was inwardly nagged by a guilty conscience for wanting to be independent in the face of what he regarded as a duty to remain with a widowed mother found himself forcibly detached from her by an impersonal draft board. He had nothing to say about it; the separation was a matter outside his control and consequently, once he was in the army, the reasons for his guilt tended to vanish. Military life conferred on him the freedom that he had long wanted but felt too guilty to seize on his own initiative, and best of all this freedom was attained under conditions of high social approval. Another, struggling honorably with the outward framework of a marriage that he held to solely because of obligation, likewise found surcease from conflict when once taken by the armed forces. A third, feeling hopelessly caught in a dull, monotonous job with no ray of hope for change, is liberated by military service and given a new lease on life. Still another, ambitious, aggressive, wanting to get ahead in the world, feels stifled in a dead-end job that offers scant opportunities for advancement. Snatched rudely but effectively into the wholly new and invigorating atmosphere of military life, with its infinite potentialities for ego recognition, he thrives like a parched plant in the rain.

Other compensations, too, are offered to many by life under military auspices. Many post-adolescents living an aimless, goalless existence in the civilian community, too immature or otherwise too lacking in motivation to take responsibility for themselves in giving shape or form or order to their lives, have this done for them in the well-ordered, well-regulated climate of army or navy. That segment of youth referred to earlier in this book as having passed their developmental years in the Depression era, with its implicit temptation to dependency, likewise may find comfortable the freedom from worry about daily existence in army life where everything is provided for them—food, shelter, clothing, entertainment—without need for reciprocal return on their part except for obedience to orders.

"Join the Navy and See the World" becomes today a slogan equally adaptable to the army, and between the two services a great part of some eleven million of our population are being given, free of charge, a glamorous Cook's tour of the world. The effects of this in the future in lessening sectionalism promise to be profound. Farm boys from Iowa match crop lore with gardeners in Italy; hillbillies from the Ozarks haggle with a dragoman at the Pyramids; secondhand shop dealers from the East Side exchange trade secrets with bazaar keepers in Bagdad; cowboys from Montana hobnob nonchalantly with tribal chiefs in the South Pacific. If one adds to this broadening experience of cosmopolitanism the related experience of breaking down caste lines within our own military forces, one sees the final results in terms of a mass maturation on the part of a huge and influential portion of our national population. It can be only speculative as to what effect this increase of maturity may have on future policies and destinies of our nation, but that there will be effects no one can doubt. It is mundane, indeed, to remark that war is a leveler of persons, but mundane or not, it is true, and the breaking down of caste lines among our troops is no small part of the compensations accruing to military life. The Midas-endowed student from Harvard's Gold Coast cannot share the danger and filth of a foxhole with the tailor from the slums without each of them coming to know better the other. The Park Avenue playboy and the sharecropper from Georgia squirming side by side on patrol in the morass of a New Guinea jungle develop a camaraderie and a mutual respect based on commonly shared, elemental danger that in most cases will outlast the experience and carry over into postwar years.

The two army psychiatrists, Drs. Maskin and Altman, whom we quoted earlier in referring to the new soldier's loss of individuality, speak of several other compensations that military life offers to certain men. These particular compensations are unique but to many are profoundly important. Reference is made to the needs of some men to prove their masculine virility, to find vicarious revenge for unconsciously held hatreds, and to establish their prestige.

"For those who have doubts about their competency as males, military service provides a means for establishing the virile role and acquiring needed reassurance. The role of hero is envisaged essentially to enhance one's sexual prestige and prowess. Implicit in this dynamism among older men is the phantasy of recaptured youth. The Peter Pan myth is the modus operandi provoking men to deeds beyond their strength in years. Viewing themselves as dashing and cutting an elegant figure in uniform, they are rejuvenated.

"War facilitates sadistic-masochistic expression. Since such behavior is sanctioned in the interests of military expediency, anxiety related to sado-masochism is mitigated. The man who has perpetrated homicide in phantasy can now externalize the act without guilt, and the masochist may seek a martyr's wounds or death. Battle provides an easy occasion for sundry displacements of hostility and killing in effigy. Hostility, originating in parental or marital conflict, for example, can be shifted on to the enemy and his destruction may symbolize vicarious revenge on wife or parents.

"War is the theatre for prestige in the making, creating numerous scenes for the emergence of new luminaries. The common man may metamorphose into the hero, and the arm-chair strategist into the warrior. Significant numbers of civilians achieve new-found distinction in positions of authority as officers, commissioned and otherwise, and concomitantly for no small number, the army provides financial rewards never previously attained. There is opportunity for special rewards, citations, decorations, honorariums, promotions, and publicity. Military advancement is definitive, readily recognized and responded to by others. In the army one can 'get somewhere.' Moreover, the acquisition of special skills and training is a vital gain from army education. Finally, military service has considerable prestige value in itself, as evidenced by the feelings of depression commonly manifested in those who are discharged. Martial ritual and ceremonials, the dress parade and brass band, provide glamor which is a significant component of self-prestige."

Entrance into military service, then, affected different personalities in different ways according pretty much to the kinds of personality equipment they took into service with them. To all, however, it was a strain of greater or lesser intensity on their capacities for adjustment, and, since a maladjusted soldier is a military liability, it became to the interests of the authorities to try to prevent or at least to lessen some of those strains. Some of the ways this was done will be explained in the following chapter.

4

HOW THE ARMY PREVENTS STRAINS OF ADJUSTMENT

IN MANY respects this war has been utterly unlike any other in history. Its action takes place at incredible speed. It is ever moving and the antithesis of the sluggish trench warfare of World War I, when opposing forces would glare at each other across a narrow strip of No Man's Land for inactive months at a time. This war has been stepped-up through newer considerations of strategy, but chiefly through the high degree of mechanization that characterizes it. Fast-moving tanks, dive bombers, rocket planes, paratroopers, commandos, six-ton block busters, concentrated rifle and machine-gun power; all these and many other innovations not only have made this war different from past ones but it has imposed quantitative and qualitative strains on its participants that never before have been paralleled. If there is a key word that differentiates this conflict from former ones, that word is "teamwork," teamwork not only between major branches of service such as army, navy, and air forces, but teamwork all the way down the chain of command to the elementary platoon. Because of this emphasis on teamwork the strains and pressures on the individual personalities making up the team have had to be carefully calculated in advance and steps taken either to lessen the strains themselves or, if that cannot be done, then to build up sturdy resistance to them. In planning for this war military authorities gave recognition to these twin needs, and one result has been the development of an elaborate system of morale maintenance.

This system operates through two approaches; one is addressed to the maintenance of morale of groups of men, while the other concentrates its activities on the individual. So far as whole groups of men are concerned good military morale can be obtained only when there is adequate knowledge of the meaning and significance of this particular war. Men must know what they are fighting for, the more concretely the better, if they are to put up with hardships, fatigue, disappointments, and frustration. Each of them in a group must become imbued with a realization that he himself is an important and valued unit in his country's war effort, if he is to carry on in the face of difficulty, which after all is the essence of morale. Military authorities realize this and have put into effect extensive programs of education that begin almost the first day the newly inducted man arrives at his training camp and continue throughout his military life. The methods of this educational program are many but its objectives are few—the crystallization of national aims and ideals, the intensification of loyalty and patriotism, and an emphasizing of the importance of the individual in a democracy.

The ways in which these objectives are attained are numerous. Since the transition from civilian to military life is usually but a few days, the lecture hall and the camp newspaper at the initial training area constitute perhaps the first orientation step. From this point on, while other specific steps are taken to indoctrinate the man, the procedure is carried out in literally hundreds of inconspicuous, nonformalized ways. For example, from general down to corporal officers deliberately endeavor to de-glamorize war and to paint instead an honest picture of military participation as an opportunity to discharge one's patriotic duty. The nature of the enemy, his psychology, his propaganda methods are described repeatedly, and the men are taught what to expect along these lines. Throughout these educational activities runs a common thread in the form of constant emphasis on the need for group identification.

But it is when the program for morale maintenance is addressed to the individual soldier that its most specific aspects are seen. In no other war in history has so much attention been paid to the individual man. This is done as a matter of economical and hardheaded business and not out of sentiment. Its purpose is to enable him to carry on long after he might otherwise be expected to give up. Part of this program is a negative process devoted to the recognition and weeding out of misfits, either actual or potential, whose instability might affect their own morale or that of their units, while another, broader part is a positive one designed to support and keep at peak efficiency the healthier men.

The weeding-out process began at the induction center, where psychiatrists skilled in recognizing the nebulous signs of potential instability or of concealed character fragility rejected from fifteen to twenty of every one hundred men reporting for examination. Many of the men so rejected could undoubtedly have become militarily useful in a protected, sheltered environment had induction-center psychiatrists been permitted to classify them for limited service, as was done in numerous borderline physical defects.

But the War Department made no provision for a limited-service classification for inductees who had borderline psychological difficulties, and, since at the time of induction no one could foresee the type of service to which such a man might be assigned, no chances were taken. Furthermore, psychiatric examination time was short (three to four minutes per man) and some latent misfits slipped through. In some areas of the country there were insufficient psychiatrists to staff the induction stations and the weeding out of the emotionally unstable had to be left to other physicians without special psychiatric training.

However, even though a potentially unstable man did slip through the meshes of the induction process now and then (and there can be no question but what many did) eagle-eyed noncoms and commissioned officers were at hand at every training camp and every receiving station to detect the early warning signals of personality maladjustment and to do something about it before it gathered much headway. The classification and assignment sections of the training camps were one of the first places where incipient maladjustment might be uncovered and dealt with by technically directed assignment to duties in accordance with the man's abilities and temperament.

The replacement training center, however, was one of the earliest proving grounds for the new soldier's abilities, and there his total personality—his emotional, intellectual, and physical qualities—came into contact with the army. Because of the strategic importance of these centers not only for military training purposes but also as places where pressures and strains on the individual soldier could be recognized and perhaps lessened, a series of unique mental hygiene clinics were organized.

The first of these was established at the Signal Corps Replacement Training Center at Fort Monmouth by Maj. Harry L. Freedman, a well-known psychiatrist. This clinic was a counterpart of the mental hygiene or psychiatric clinics that have become commonplace in many communities throughout the country. It was staffed by the usual clinical team of psychiatrists, psychiatric social workers, and clinical psychologists, and it performed the same functions as civilian clinics do: *i.e.*, attempted to *prevent* early disorders of personality or behavior from becoming severe rather than to undertake the treatment or cure of full-blown ones. In terse military language Major Freedman sets forth the purposes of this mental hygiene unit in an article published in *Mental Hygiene*, the quarterly journal of the National Committee for Mental Hygiene as follows:

"The mission of the Mental Hygiene Unit is:

(a) To provide mental hygiene facilities to organizations and officers and assist them with soldiers who present various forms of maladjustment such as inaptitude, unusual behavior, malingering ('gold-bricking'), recalcitrance, alcoholism, and others.

(b) To institute such corrective measures as are considered appropriate to reduce or eliminate the individual's

maladjustment and eradicate factors related to the incipient causes of mental breakdown to the extent necessary for
the soldier to perform military duties.

(c) To determine whether an individual whose case is
brought to the Unit for attention, is either in an assignment that does not utilize his capacities to the fullest possible extent, or is being trained in a skill beyond his capacity.

(d) To recommend for discharge from the service such
men, who because of emotional or mental factors cannot
function adequately or who present a hazard to other men.

(e) To provide psychiatric, psychological and social
data and make recommendations to courts-martial and discharge boards.

(f) To aid soldiers who are discharged from the service
to make the transition back to civilian life."

As will be seen from a reading of the above, the sole concern of the military forces is to find and to keep men fit for
fighting a war. His military usefulness is the only criterion
for retaining a man in service. If he is maladjusted to merely
a minor extent, every effort is made to remedy the condition
and salvage him for continued duty. If the maladjustment is
severe and if its correction is unlikely or if it promises to take
too much time to remedy it, then outright discharge from
military service is the rule.

Illustrative of the method of reassignment recommended
sometimes by the Mental Hygiene Unit as a means of cor-
recting a "round peg in a square hole" situation is the following:

Private F., a twenty-four-year-old soldier of average intelligence and eighth-grade education, who had been a cow-puncher in civilian life, was referred to the mental-hygiene unit after a long hospitalization because he had been placed in limited service due to a knee injury acquired while in action. He was disturbed over his physical condition and inclined to put all the responsibility for it upon the army. With some encouragement, however, he could take part in the task of locating a job placement for him, in which, despite his disability, he could function usefully. As the interviewer considered with him how his experience might be used in the army, he brought out an interest in horses and skills in harness work. The unit then got into contact with the officer in charge of the post stables and arranged an interview. The soldier, at first frightened by the prospect of the interview, was given encouragement by the interviewer. After the interview, he was accepted for assignment to the stables. The worker saw the soldier periodically and helped him with his problem of getting back to a definite job after a long period of disability. His knowledge of horses and harness work gained him recognition on the job and advancement to the rank of technician, fifth grade.

Still another case shows how the Mental Hygiene Unit co-operates with court-martial boards in disciplinary cases.

Private L. was referred to the unit for evaluation and recommendation in regard to his having been A.W.O.L. At the unit, the social worker learned from him that he had been to the city, had drunk excessively, and could not regain control of himself until after he had been A.W.O.L.

for several days. He had been drinking heavily for the last four years and had several times been on the verge of delirium tremens. Field investigation indicated that the soldier had been making an adequate adjustment in his company, except for his A.W.O.L. incident, and was qualifying in the specialized school that he was attending. Psychological examination indicated that he had sufficient capacity to qualify as a skilled technician, if he could concentrate on his training. Further investigation of his home background was initiated. A report of his civilian adjustment was received from the Red Cross, which verified his losing jobs frequently and being hospitalized numerous times because of alcoholism. This report, taken together with the fact that the soldier had again gone A.W.O.L., made it clear that he could not be relied upon to control his habitual drinking for more than short periods of time. He was recommended for discharge because of chronic alcoholism, and such action was effected.

Another court-martial case had a happier ending and illustrates how the Red Cross cooperates with the Mental Hygiene Unit to preserve a soldier for useful service.

Private D., aged twenty, of average intelligence, was referred because he was A.W.O.L. for the second time. The soldier had married just prior to induction. His wife was pregnant and had been living with his family. The family now had forced the soldier's wife out of their home. She had moved in with her married sister, but she was in poor health because of her pregnancy and was not able to get adequate care. Concern over his wife led the soldier to go

A.W.O.L., the only way in which he believed he could assist her in getting medical care. Discussion with him of Red Cross facilities resulted in a reference of the case to the Red Cross worker in the unit, who was able to effect liaison between the soldier and his wife. Plans were made for regular contacts between the Red Cross worker and the soldier in which information could be exchanged and plans worked out to help him overcome some of his anxiety about the home situation. The wife was interviewed by a Red Cross worker in the city, guided in her problem, and provided with medical care. The soldier felt relieved and has been able to continue with full effort in his training and assignment.

Weeding out the misfits is a vital part of the military program of morale maintenance. Such individuals not only are inefficient themselves but they tend to require a disproportionate amount of their officers' time, and some, depending on the nature of their attitudes, breed discontent among their fellows. Their early recognition and separation from the service becomes, then, a matter of real importance to the efficacy of their unit as a whole. One particular kind of misfit is found in what is called the "psychopathic personality." Such individuals are to be found in substantial numbers in every community and every large military unit and they constitute one of the most puzzling and vexing problems with which society has to deal. These persons are not insane in any legal sense, nor do most of them possess subnormal intelligence. Indeed, many are of definitely superior intellectual attainments. But they display a defect in character formation that in most cases defies the skill of modern science to fill in. Psychiatric textbooks contain many descriptions of the psychopathic personality, but perhaps one of the most illuminating is painted in a circular distributed by the War Department itself among physicians at various induction stations throughout the country.

"Psychopathic personalities:—In this ill-defined, more or less heterogeneous group are placed those individuals who, although not suffering from a congenital defect in the intellectual sphere, do manifest a definite defect in their ability to profit by experience. They are unable to proceed through life with any definite pattern of standardized activity. They are unable to respond in an adult social manner to the demands of honesty, truthfulness, decency, and consideration of their fellow associates. They are emotionally unstable, not to be depended upon; act impulsively with poor judgment; are always in difficulties, have many and various schemes without logical basis, lack tenacity of purpose, are easily influenced and oftentimes in conflict with the law. They do not take kindly to regimentation and are continually at variance with those who attempt to indoctrinate them in the essentials of military discipline. Such an individual has a decided influence upon his fellow associates and the morale of his organization, for he will not conform himself to organized authority and he derives much satisfaction in cultivating insubordination in others. Quite frequently he presents a favorable impression, is neat in appearance, talks well, and is well mannered. However, under this veneer the real defect is evident by past irresponsiveness to social demands and lack of continuity of purpose. Among this general group are to be placed many

homosexuals, grotesque and pathological liars, vagabonds, wanderers, the inadequate and emotionally unstable, petty offenders, swindlers, kleptomaniacs, pyromaniacs, alcoholics, and likewise those highly irritable and arrogant individuals, so-called pseudoquerulents, 'guard-house lawyers,' who are forever critical of organized authority and imbued with feelings of abuse and lack of consideration by their fellow men. All such men should be excluded from the service as far as possible, both because of the difficulties which these symptoms themselves cause and because of the fact that such individuals ultimately may develop fullfledged psychotic states."

Military reports from all fronts are replete with instances of combat catastrophes and lowering of company morale caused by the psychopathic personality, and his discharge from service as soon as recognized becomes of paramount importance. Unfortunately, on his return to his home town the "psychopath" continues to be the same psychopathic personality he was before he ever entered the army, and he constitutes a goodly percentage of the chronic troublemakers, the "gripers," the malcontents who may cast a stigma on the whole group of ex-servicemen in any community. After the last war not a few such psychopaths utilized their aggressiveness and external plausibility to force their way into responsible positions in ex-servicemen's organizations, where their innate habit of troublemaking created friction and dissension. So far as treatment or cure of such individuals is concerned, neither psychiatry nor any other scientific skill has much hope to offer in their present stage of development. "Once a psychopathic personality, always a psychopath" seems to be the rule, and such personalities promise to continue to be thorns in the side of the community indefinitely.

The Mental Hygiene Units described in the preceding pages were not the only methods devised to lessen some of the strains of adjustment to military life of the new soldier, and consequently to prevent a number of later breakdowns. The man in whom you are interested may have been assigned to an organization where the Advisor System was in effect. This unique system, under the direction of Maj. S. H. Kraines, an army psychiatrist, was initiated in the Tank Destroyer Replacement Training Center at North Camp Hood, Texas, in 1943. Its purpose was to enhance military efficiency and it operated on preventive lines, dealing with individual maladjustment and with group morale. The situations for which it was organized are told in Major Kraines's [1] own words:

"Many men who enter have problems related to their dislocation from civilian routine and to their adjustment to military service. In addition, there are innumerable men who were poorly adjusted in their previous relatively stable community life and whose induction into the army precipitates a host of personal difficulties of an emotional nature. Some of the problems are easily solved; some are much more difficult, perhaps the most difficult being those that stem from the basic instability of the trainee.

"Where can the soldier turn for help? The army provides a method. According to the 'Soldier's Handbook,' if a man wishes to see his company commander, all he need do

[1] "The Advisor System—Prophylactic Psychiatry on a Mass Scale," *Mental Hygiene*, October, 1943.

is request permission from the first sergeant. Every company commander, in the interests of his own unit, exerts continual effort to ferret out those cases that need help, but as in any large organization, the plan and ideal are occasionally frustrated. It sounds simple; but in actual working practice it is occasionally difficult and involved. Investigation of several cases of men suffering from severe emotional stresses revealed that they had not sought help through channels, and being shy and reticent, they gave up in either disgust or hopelessness. Any delay in the solution of a problem arouses varying degrees of disgust, despair, or defiance. Curbstone advice adds to the confusion. Moreover, the shy and sensitive man, who is often the one most in need of help, finds it difficult, if not impossible, to expose his personal anxiety to so many different persons; he would rather 'suffer in silence.' As a consequence, the army also suffers through the decreased efficiency of the soldier, his loss of ability to concentrate, and so on. It is easy for disgruntled, disappointed, or distraught men to assume the attitude of, 'To hell with the army! It isn't interested in me; why should I be interested in it?' It is difficult for commanders to appreciate the existence of this spirit when their men parade smartly in review; but if it exists, it is a hindrance in training and a definite danger in combat situation.

"Too often the trainees get 'the brush off'—evasive, noncommittal answers from noncommissioned officers who are either indifferent or powerless to help in a particular situation. Too often the sergeant, who is responsible for discipline and who has many urgent and time-consuming duties, is brief and brusque in his answers. Too often, conditioned and well-adjusted army men dismiss as trivia the problems that to the raw recruit are of paramount importance. Too often, in the absence of any easily accessible source of information, fantastic misinformation in the form of wild rumors is spread.

"There are countless manifestations of this spirit of disquiet and emotional turmoil over unresolved problems. Some trainees develop neurotic difficulties, and 'ride the sick book' to the point of interfering with training; some leave camp without permission and become subject to disciplinary action; some wreak great harm by communicating to others their spirit of indifference or rebellion; some even attempt suicide. Inevitably the morale of the whole group is lowered by the disaffection of its constituent members."

To deal with this situation the Advisor System utilized the services of specially trained noncommissioned officers. Noncoms were chosen purposely on the basis that they lived in the same barracks with the trainees, were associated with them continuously during the training period, and consequently came to know them with a degree of intimacy impossible for the commanding officer to establish. Trainees with "problems" were encouraged to "talk it out" with these selected noncoms, who were assigned to such service because of possession of the following qualifications:

"(1) Sufficient army experience so that they 'know the ropes'; (2) capacity for common-sense judgment; (3) interest in the work of advising; (4) maturity, usually found in men somewhat older than the average trainee, that will inspire confidence; and (5) 'popularity'—that is, the kind of personality that expresses and readily evokes friendliness."

The program was in no sense one of pampering or coddling. On the contrary, its whole purpose was so to toughen men that they achieved their highest potential military efficiency. Major Kraines cites several case histories to illustrate something of the variety of the problems for which the noncoms acted as advisors and to demonstrate the techniques of solution of those problems.

"A soldier who was extremely disturbed emotionally came to his advisor and told him that he was 'beside himself' with worry over what he could do about his mother, who was insane. Discussion revealed that the mother had been placed in a state mental institution. After extended discussion between the advisor and the trainee, it became obvious that the best possible solution for the mother was to be in the asylum and that the trainee could in no way aid her. However, because the soldier was not completely satisfied, an interview with the company commander was arranged. Substantially the same suggestions that the advisor had made were given by the company commander. Private A, who was sympathetically treated and who was given an honest evaluation of his problem, was able to make an excellent adjustment instead of having a continuous emotional disturbance that would have impaired his efficiency as a soldier."

"Private B, whose wife was due to have a child, requested an emergency furlough; but because of the war situation at the time, the request was denied. This denial was a severe disappointment to the soldier, who began to drink beer at the post exchange to such an extent that he would come to the barracks intoxicated. The advisor undertook to look after him. He talked with him frequently and went along with him on the beer-drinking expeditions. As a result of conversations with the advisor, Private B 'woke up' to the futility of his behavior and 'snapped out of it.' He became personally loyal to the advisor and thereafter made a good adjustment as a soldier. A significant side-light in this case is that the advisor, who had previously been regarded as a 'hard-boiled old army man,' improved tremendously as a result of his advisory experience. He developed greater sympathy and understanding for his platoon and curbed certain bullying tendencies that previously had been pronounced."

"One soldier had a great deal of difficulty in drill, marching, and 'doing double-time.' Although he had gone on sick call, the initial examination had revealed no outstanding pathology, and the soldier was ordered to return to full duty. The advisor was convinced that Private E was neither neurotic nor malingering and referred the case through the company commander to the psychiatric consultant. The psychiatrist ascertained the fact that Private E had had in childhood a fever that was followed by prolonged weakness of the muscles of the legs. Orthopedic consultation, which was arranged for, established the fact that this boy had suffered from infantile poliomyelitis and reclassification for limited service was arranged."

"The advisor referred Private *F* through the company commander to the psychiatric consultant. Private *F* had been in the company for ten days and had eaten only two meals during that time. He had not complained and had continued in his regular activities with the other trainees. It was only because the advisor was cognizant of the individual habits of the men in his section that the case was reported. On examination it was found that Private *F* was suffering from an early schizophrenic psychosis; that he performed his duties mechanically; that he was not interested in food; that he 'fantasied' greatly; and that he was suffering from the feeling of persecution. Private *F* was referred to the neuropsychiatric ward for further study."

To some these situations may seem trivial and unworthy of large-scale methods of treatment. Military experience, however, has demonstrated over and over again that such apparently minor situations when continued without abatement and when multiplied by a score or more of similar situations in each unit are capable of affecting for the worse the morale of whole groups. These simple, common-sense methods of treatment are easily invoked in military as well as in civilian life and the experience of the Advisor System amply demonstrates their worth.

The foregoing offers an admittedly rough picture of why it is that no nation has ever done more than ours to build and maintain the morale of its fighting men, both in groups and in individuals. That it has paid handsome dividends is apparent from the never-ending stream of official reports of combat efforts carried on long after less well-prepared men would have given up. The amazing success of an army made up mostly of recent civilians in resisting the strains of warfare could not have been achieved without the elaborate programs of morale maintenance described in the preceding pages.

Despite these efforts, however, the sobering fact remains that considerable numbers of men did break down in military service. Some broke physically, but as many or more broke psychologically. Some broke at training camps early in the game, while others broke only under the continued impact of the unspeakable horrors of actual battle. The breakdowns of some were slight, of others severe.

Excluding the battle-wounded, however, and those whose illness was purely physical, the majority of men who broke down in military service suffered from one of the many disorders coming under the heading of "psychiatric." In recent years, and especially since the outbreak of the war, this term is seeing frequent usage. No longer is it confined to the pages of medical textbooks, for the intelligent layman has routinely included it in his everyday vocabulary. Nevertheless, to many it still carries some mysterious, half-fearful meaning, and, since misconception about the term is rife and since if it is incorrectly interpreted it is apt to bring unmerited alarm or stigma, we shall see in the next chapter just what a "psychiatric handicap" really is.

5

SOLDIERS WITH PSYCHIATRIC DISABILITIES

WHAT *is* this much-talked-about condition, a psychiatric disability, that is responsible for nearly half of all medical discharges from military service? One wishes that a simple, accurate, and concise definition could be offered. Unfortunately, the matter is so complicated that no such simplicity has yet been achieved. Perhaps the best that can be done—and even this is over-simplification—is to say that a psychiatric condition can be thought of as an impairment of some part (or the *function* of some part) of the equipment that helps us adjust to different experiences. As a result of this impairment we become less happy or less efficient than otherwise might be the case.

But if we do not know how to define the term concisely at least we can explain something about it, even though this volume is in no sense a medical textbook. Suppose we try to strip it of some of its mysteriousness and look at it this way: In the first place, all our life from the day we are born might be thought of as a process of having to adjust ourselves to one thing after another. Some of the things that necessitate adjustment lie in the external world, while others come from deep within ourselves. But adjust we must, in some fashion or other, and the fashions in which we do it are labeled by society as "healthy" or "unhealthy," depending on whether or not they promote acceptable living.

Thus, we find ourselves required to adjust to heat, to cold; to sickness, to deformity; to people who like us and to those who don't; to authority; to secret fears of our own adequacy; to our limitations and temperaments; to disappointments; to threats to our self-esteem; and sometimes to dangers to our very lives. Nature furnished us with three interlocking sets of equipment with which to make these adjustments: (1) our physical bodies, with their organs and methods of functioning, (2) our individual quota of that quality called "intelligence," and (3) our emotions (or, if you prefer, our feelings). These three equipments were designed originally to dovetail into each other and to operate as one harmonious whole, and all together they go to make up what is termed our "total personality." When they do function harmoniously we are said to be well adjusted. No one of these equipments can be detached or lifted out of the matrix of the whole and treated as a separate, isolated unit. If something happens to one piece of this adjusting equipment, the chances are that the others also may be thrown out of balance to some degree.

The great integrating system of the body—the Great Adjuster—that permits all its internal parts to operate as an effective whole and that helps adjust the total person to the demands of his environment is the nervous system. This is an extremely delicate apparatus whose operative function is not unlike that of the gyroscope stabilizer attached to the controls of an airplane. Sometimes a strong wind tends to push the plane off its level course. The gyroscope goes into action and by automatically manipulating the controls sets the plane once more back onto its proper course. Perhaps a downdraft sucks the plane dangerously near jagged mountain peaks below; or maybe a vicious air current sends it climbing at such a steep pitch that a stall or a tail spin is imminent. But if the gyroscope is on the job it readjusts the controls so that level flight is again achieved and the plane proceeds on its mission efficiently. This is, in a sense, what the nervous system does in helping us to adjust to the forces that impinge against us and threaten to send us crashing unless we can right ourselves.

Once in a while, however, a gyroscope is not on the job and disaster overtakes the plane because an occasional instrument leaves the factory with a hidden flaw or concealed weakness that escaped the inspector's attention. Once in a while, also, disaster overtakes a person in making an adjustment to a certain experience because he may have come into the world with a nervous system that was defective in some way or was otherwise unsuitable from the beginning for the job which it was called on to perform. When these weaknesses in original structure are present both the defective gyroscope and the defective nervous system are apt to break down if some unusual strain is placed upon them.

Of course, if the plane encounters no powerful cross winds, and if the owner of the nervous system gets into (or can make for himself) an environment where he need not be faced with the necessity for adjusting to any difficult experiences, all goes placidly and the hidden flaws never appear. But cross winds in the air and difficult experiences in life are the rule rather than the exception, and sooner or later the plane or the owner of a nervous system with a concealed structural fragility is likely to meet with some unusual condition that calls for unusual efforts at adjustment. Then the resulting strain on the adjusting machinery may become so great that the weakened apparatus is unequal to the task of absorbing that strain, and the resulting behavior of the machine as a whole becomes erratic, undependable, or inefficient.

Some difficulties in adjusting to various experiences in life are due, therefore, to flaws in the original structure of the nervous system of certain individuals. More commonly encountered, however, are nervous systems that originally were sound and free from flaws but that, nevertheless, caused trouble for their owners in adjusting because of the unsuitable ways in which they were "set" or broken in during that process of training in childhood which corresponds to the test flight of an airplane.

Almost everyone knows that before the new model of a bomber is sent on its first real mission the pilot takes it up for a test flight in order to get acquainted with its intricacies and to see how efficiently it performs the special service for which it was built. On its return to the ground it is placed in the hands of skilled mechanics, who straighten out the kinks revealed in the test flight, which also demonstrated to the pilot that he must change some of his methods of manipulating if he wishes to get the best results out of this particular plane. Perhaps the test flight taught him that this bomber, in contrast to another of the same type, tends to veer a bit to the left; or that under certain conditions he must feed it more gas than would be necessary for some other plane; or possibly that this one for some unrecognized reason is an excessively sensitive plane, reacting overviolently to every gust of wind out of the ordinary; that for peak performance a light touch here and a heavy one there is the proper management. From what he learns in this test flight the pilot is enabled to set the gyroscope of that particular plane to adjust to most of the things that might occur to it, although the setting he gives the instrument might be all wrong for the twin sister of that plane.

For closely similar reasons the nervous system of an individual must be properly "set" or conditioned at the beginning of life's long flight (*i.e.*, during the formative years of childhood) if the person is to adjust suitably to the different experiences that life is certain to bring to him. This is why the processes of child training are comparable to the test flights of the airplane.

When an adult is faced with the need for adjusting to some experience that comes to him either from the outside world or from within himself, the success with which he makes that adjustment is more likely to depend on the kind of habits or patterns he formed in the past in meeting similar experiences than it is on any defect in the structure of his nervous system. These habits or patterns are formed in the child pretty much as a result of the way his parents train him. Both for parents and for children it is apt to be a sort of trial-and-error process. Children not less than adults have to adjust to many experiences each day, but to them the experiences are new and much experimenting has to be done to find ways of adjusting to them. To an adult, on the other hand, experiences that require adjusting to are "old stuff" (simply because the adult has lived longer and has met more of them), and he does not have to do quite so much experimenting with ways of adjustment because by this time the habits or patterns for meeting them that he evolved during childhood have now become automatic, *i.e.*, the same general type of experience automatically elicits the same general type of response.

An example may make this clearer. A six-year-old child asks for a second piece of cake at supper. His mother refuses him and in so doing creates one of those life experiences we have been discussing. This particular experience in itself is not very important, but it is a forerunner of a type of experience that the boy is going to meet innumerable times as long as he lives: *i.e.*, the experience of encountering and having to adjust to *frustration* of some of his desires.

Of course, frustration is only one of a number of the basic experiences in life that were discussed in Chap. 2, and, like all experiences, it can be mild or it can be severe. The point is, however, that the first few times any new experience is encountered we experiment with methods of dealing with it, and, when we finally devise one that to us seems satisfactory, we tend to use that same method every time we meet a similar kind of experience.

Suppose we see how this works out in the case of the boy previously mentioned. In response to his mother's refusal of the second piece of cake he may not give in gracefully to this frustration of his desire. Being an averagely determined youngster, he tries to outsmart the frustration and perhaps selects the device of a temper tantrum as the way to do it. He screams, he lies down on the floor and kicks, and he holds his breath until he is blue in the face. By means of this behavior he hopes to get around the frustration and force his mother to give in by frightening her with the threat of his suffocating, or by embarrassing her into yielding through staging the tantrum when the bridge club is meeting, or possibly by the age-old childhood method of sheer wearing her down through incessant whining and teasing. If, as a result of the boy's tantrum, his mother does give in and he gets the second piece of cake, then he would indeed be less than clever if he failed to try the same device the next time he met the experience of being frustrated in something. And if the tantrum device works successfully the second and the third and the fourth time, the boy need experiment no longer. He has discovered a way of adjusting to the experience of frustration that serves his ends, and soon it becomes an automatic habit or pattern every time he encounters this particular difficulty in life. Nor does he usually abandon this habit or outgrow it as he gets older. Why should he, so long as it continues to function? He carries it with him from childhood into adolescence, and from that stage of his development into adult years, when by this time it has been incorporated into the very structure of his personality.

Of course, as the boy grows older he makes changes in the outward appearance of the tantrum. He learns, for example, that at sixteen one does not lie down on the floor and scream and kick as one did at six, but that there are appropriate disguises that may bring the same results. He learns, further, that at twenty-six an adolescent manner of staging a tantrum needs revision into an adult equivalent. But regardless of the way in which it is expressed it is the same old device he learned to use in childhood, and so long as it still continues to influence people into giving-in to him he would not be sensible to discard it. Now by the time he has become an adult he has learned to adjust to the experience of frustration by outsmarting it with a special type of behavior, namely, a temper tantrum, no matter how cleverly disguised, and whenever he meets with frustration he automatically resorts to this method. In other words, he has developed a habit or pattern of adjustment that he will endeavor to carry through life with him so long as people will give in to it as his mother did.

A crude tantrum is only one of many ways of dealing with some frustration of our desires. Instead, we can, if we think it stands a better chance of succeeding, sulk and pout in the hope of making the person who frustrates us feel sorry and give in; or we can retreat into a hurt silence and brood and try to punish the person by not speaking for a day or two; or we can accuse him of not liking us, of discriminating against us, or of just plain wanting to be mean to us. It makes little difference what method we unconsciously select to combat the frustration so long as it works. The meaning and also the purpose of the behavior are identical no matter what guise it takes.

Like many other apparently successful modes of behavior in life there is a catch in this temper-tantrum method. Because it worked so successfully during childhood when it was used against the family who loved him, and because by this time this particular way of adjusting to the experience of frustration had become a habit, the adult naturally expects it will work with equal success against other people. Here is where the catch comes in. Sooner or later (and for his own ultimate good we hope sooner) he encounters a frustration at the hands of someone who does not particularly love him; who, indeed, may not care a rap about him. Worse yet, the frustration may come, not from a person at all, but from some immovable impersonal fact in life, like being separated (through death or distance) from an overprotective, pampering mother on whom he still retains an infantile dependency; or having insufficient money for a college education; or having to submit to a painful surgical operation; or being refused enlistment in the army because of weak eyes or a damaged heart, etc., ad infinitum.

When the boy or the adult he may have grown into meets the stone wall of frustrations like these he is bewildered. Here at last is an experience in life that refuses to yield, as his mother did, to the tried and proven habit of a tantrum. Neither the frontal assaults of rages and storming nor the flank attacks of pouting and sulking budge the experience an inch. The oversolicitous mother to whom he was attached in such infantile fashion and who subsequently died will not return to life in response to his most frantic appeals to her sympathy; the weak heart that keeps him out of the army will not miraculously become strong no matter how he blusters at the induction center doctor; and the needed surgical operation will not become unneeded as a result of his raging denials. He is bewildered, he is angry, *but most of all he is afraid.* His former sense of omnipotence is threatened; his delusion that he could proceed gaily through life always sidestepping frustration through use of his tantrum device is shattered, and since perhaps he had never learned any other method he becomes filled with anxiety.

If this man's immutable frustration is, after all, not too important, his resulting anxiety may be only mild and merely annoying instead of incapacitating. But if the frustration happens to be one of vital significance to him, or if his former pattern of dealing with it had become so deeply embedded in his personality that this had grown rigid and inflexible, then his anxiety may mount to a panic that cripples his social and personal effectiveness in direct ratio to its intensity.

With this roundabout preamble we are now ready to get back to the discussion of "what is a psychiatric condition?" with which this chapter was opened. It was suggested that a psychiatric condition could be thought of as an impairment of some part (or the *function* of some part) of the equipment that helps us adjust to different experiences, so that as a result of this impairment we become less happy or less efficient than otherwise might be the case. Further, it was pointed out that the nervous system is the integrating force that helps various parts of our adjusting equipment to operate harmoniously and thus to keep us well-adjusted people.

When the boy cited as an example finally met with an experience of frustration that refused to yield to the only method of persuasion he knew, an impairment of part of his adjusting machinery was brought about; the feelings of anger and anxiety that arose out of being thwarted caused him to become less happy than he might have been had he been permitted to learn healthier ways of dealing with frustration through wiser methods of child training, and the behavior he used as a means of expressing those feelings caused his personal and social adjustment to become likewise less satisfactory. In other words, the boy found himself suffering from a psychiatric condition.

But, readers may object, how can this be? Does not the word "psychiatric" refer to insanity? And, surely, the boy discussed is not insane? Of course he is not insane, and the chances are he will never become so, but a psychiatric condition describes a multitude of departures from average happiness and efficiency of less severity than insanity. After all, if someone tells us that Frank Smith is sick, we do not necessarily jump to the conclusion that he has tuberculosis or cancer. He might merely be a little unhappy and less able than usual to concentrate on his work because he is all stuffed up from a cold in the head. In a few days, probably, he will be as well as ever, provided that complications do not set in. So also may the boy's psychiatric condition clear up after a bit, again provided that complications do not arise in the form of an experience too frustrating for his equipment to adjust to, or provided that his personality is not too rigid to adapt. Just as there are many kinds of physical sickness, so are there many varieties of psychiatric ones. For every psychiatric condition so malignant as to deserve the label "insanity" there are hundreds of others ranging upward in mildness to mere prejudices, quirks, or sensitivities so inconspicuous as to pass almost unnoticed. Nevertheless, in a technical sense at least even the mildest of these conditions represents some impairment of its owner's happiness and efficiency as a social unit and therefore fulfills the sketchy requirements that constitute a psychiatric condition.

Not only are there many, many different *kinds* of psychiatric conditions, but they masquerade under many different guises. One (a very severe one) may appear as insanity. Another may be expressed as more-than-average moodiness or gloominess or chronic suspiciousness. A third may adopt the disguise of physical symptoms that mislead the owner— and others, too, for that matter—into believing he has heart disease or stomach disease or some other organic trouble. Still another may manifest itself as a compulsion to step on every crack in the sidewalk or to count fence pickets or to wash the hands a certain number of times. Then there are other kinds of psychiatric disorders that emerge in the form of antisocial behavior, such as certain instances of delinquency, crime, and other unethical practices.

Over and above all these are myriad other disguises for psychiatric disorders so (apparently) within the bounds of normality that few ever think of them as having a psychiatric significance. For example, there is the man who has a prejudice against redheaded people so strong—if illogical—that he prefers to limp along in the office with an incompetent black-haired secretary than to hire an efficient red-haired one. There is the woman whose friends dread to visit her because they have learned that her feelings are so inordinately sensitive that they are always being hurt; she reads slights and innuendoes into every conversation and is perpetually certain that people are aiming to take advantage of her. Then we have the man whose secret feelings of inferiority cause him to develop a protective outer manner of pugnacity, a chip-on-the-shoulder philosophy toward others, and a cruel ruthlessness designed to get the best of the other fellow before the latter gets the best of him.

These are but microscopic fragments of the attitudes many people carry through life with them, which make them a little less happy than they might be and a little less efficient as good citizens and neighbors. The owners of these little peculiarities of personality as well as their friends would be indignant were their mannerisms to be labeled as "psychiatric." Nevertheless, the unpalatable fact must be faced that within the meaning of the explanation in this chapter these mild peculiarities have come into being as an expression of some impairment of the owner's adjusting equipment and therefore are psychiatric despite the manner of their disguise.

The *causes* for psychiatric disorders likewise vary as much as the causes for physical ones. Typhoid fever has a different cause from an ulcer of the stomach, and clogged-up sinuses are likely to have little in common with the origins of varicose veins. By the same token, the causes for general paresis are utterly different from the causes of schizophrenia (two of the different severe psychiatric conditions or insanities). And the processes of aging that precipitate senile dementia are apt to be quite different from those that cause a man to develop an alcoholic psychosis.

Not all, by any means, of the causes for psychiatric conditions have been discovered as yet, and for the originating factor in some we are as much in the dark as we are at this stage of scientific knowledge about the causes for cancer. Some psychiatric conditions are caused by—or, at least, are accompanied by—physical diseases or alterations of physical processes. General paresis, just mentioned, is one of these, and is caused by syphilis of the central nervous system, in which actual damage to brain structure can be demonstrated on autopsy. Delirium tremens resulting from long-continued and excessive use of alcohol is another. The second-childhood and the vagaries of memory and mood of the senile who suffers from hardening of the arteries of the brain is still a third.

Where the cause for a psychiatric condition is known to result from some physical disease, we call it an "organic" psychiatric condition. Most psychiatric conditions, however, do not spring from any discoverable physical cause although sometimes their symptoms partake of a physical coloring.

Where no physical cause can be demonstrated a psychiatric condition is labeled as "functional," *i.e.*, the function of part or all of the total personality, rather than the physical structure of an organ, is impaired. The overwhelming majority of soldiers who return from military service with some psychiatric condition suffer from one of these functional types of disorder without actual physical or organic involvement.

If the causes for psychiatric disorders and their grades of severity differ as much as physical disorders do, it will be seen that the treatment likewise must vary as widely. The treatment of appendicitis is not the same as for tuberculosis, nor is the treatment of schizophrenia (dementia praecox) very much like the treatment of general paresis. Since the precise cause for numerous psychiatric conditions is not yet known, treatment often has to be limited to treatment of the symptoms that the condition has aroused. This is not scientific medicine, to be sure, but it is the best we can do with our present knowledge, and it must be admitted that even treatment of symptoms results astonishingly often in relief.

The technical language used in describing psychiatric disorders adds to the layman's confusion about the whole subject. *Schizophrenia, manic-depressive, psychoneurosis, obsessive-compulsive states, superego, oligophrenia*—these are all tongue twisters that seem strange and mysterious, largely because psychiatry is one of the youngest of the medical specialities and its terminology has not yet had time to become incorporated into the vocabulary of the layman (or, for that matter, of a good many physicians). But perhaps in time *schizophrenia* or *psychoneurosis* or *conversion hysteria* may become as commonplace words in the verbal equipment of the man in the street as tuberculosis or poliomyelitis or arthritis.

In the meantime, few of these technical terms need be used in everyday conversation if we limit ourselves to describing behavior instead of attempting to pin complicated diagnostic labels on the conditions that produce the behavior. One possible exception to this may be the word "psychoneurosis," which has been bandied about so extensively in World War II. Psychiatrists themselves have differing definitions and differing understandings of this term, which depend on what type of psychiatric training they have had. Most of them, however, restrict psychoneurosis to a special kind of nervous disorder in which conflict between warring parts of the unconscious mind (for example, conflict between the ego and the repressed forces of the libido) is the principal causative factor. Among the general public, however, the term "psychoneurosis" is a scrap-basket term into which is dumped almost any and every kind of psychiatric condition, from the severest insanity to the mildest eccentricity of personality. In military usage it threatens to become the current substitute for the outmoded and abandoned "shell shock" of 1918. For practical purposes, therefore, it has come to mean nothing at all and in everyday conversation might well be discarded. This has been made easier to do since military authorities in the spring of 1944 officially dropped the term "psychoneurosis" on the discharge papers of men about to be separated from military service because of some psychiatric condition and substituted instead the much more sensible phrase "unsuited for military service."

There is at present a widespread but cruelly unjustified stigma with which so many otherwise kindly and intelligent persons surround any aspect of the word "psychiatric." This quite unmerited stigma causes the families of many persons who are ill with a mental disorder to adopt a "hush-hush" attitude in public about the sick man. If his illness is of a type that can best be treated in a special hospital for such disorders, the family are evasive when asked where the patient has gone. Perhaps they reply that he is visiting relatives and taking a rest or maybe they say he has entered some general hospital for a checkup. All too frequently they lack the courage to tell the truth: that he has become sick with a sickness whose symptoms are in the realm of the mind rather than exclusively of the body and that, like any sensible person whose illness stands a better chance of getting well by going to a hospital, he has entered a psychiatric hospital for the special treatment he needs.

There is no more disgrace in having a mental illness than a physical one. True, a vicious old legend would have it that a mental disorder (*i.e.*, a psychiatric one) points to a skeleton in the family closet of heredity or that it somehow indicates a shameful weakness of will on the part of the patient. Indeed, unbelievable as it may sound, there are still many people who sincerely remain under the influence of that medieval superstition that an insane person is one whose mind has been taken possession of by demons or evil spirits. After all, insanity is merely one of many different varieties of psychiatric illness. It is a legal, not a medical, term, and all it means is that the man or woman so labeled has a type of illness severe enough to affect his judgment and his behavior to a degree that makes it desirable for others to take over his decisions for him. This is done by means of a legal process known as "commitment," which gives him his chance to get well in a suitable hospital. The process of commitment is often necessary because the patient's disordered state of mind may so affect his judgment that he does not know what is best for him and consequently may resist hospital treatment.

As was indicated in preceding pages, a great many people display some type of mental or psychiatric disorder, but in only about one out of twenty of these does this disorder merit the name of "insanity." "A *disorder is a mental disorder if its roots are mental*," said the late Dr. C. Macfie Campbell, professor of psychiatry at Harvard Medical School.[1] Dr. Campbell goes on to say:

". . . a headache indicates a mental disorder if it comes because one is dodging something disagreeable. A pain in the back is a mental disorder if its persistence is due to discouragement and a desire to have a sick benefit, rather than to put one's back into one's work. Sleeplessness is a mental disorder if its basis lies in personal worries and emotional tangles. . . . Discontent with one's environment is a mental disorder if its cause lies, not in some external situation but in personal failure to deal with one's own emotional problems. Suspicion, distrust, misinterpretation: all these are mental disorders when they are the disguised expression of repressed longings into which the person has no clear insight. Stealing sometimes indicates a mental disorder: the odd expression of under-lying conflicts in the person's mind, or of discouragement, inability to meet situations, lack of interest in the opportunities available. . . . Unsociability, marital incompatibility, alcohol-

[1] *Modern Conception of Mental Disorder*, Harvard University Press, Cambridge, Mass.

ism, an aggressive, embittered social attitude; all these and more may indicate a disorder of mental balance which may be open to modification."

It will be seen from what has just been said by Dr. Campbell that few if any of these manifestations of mental disorder can be considered as evidence of insanity, even though they all fall within the classification of "mental." Suppose we look further and see what kind of people display these mental disorders. Says Dr. Campbell in continuing:

". . . We have now reviewed the sort of human material which is before us when we try to frame a general conception of mental disorders. It is a variegated group. It includes respectable bankers peevish with their wives; scrupulous house-wives with immaculate—and uncomfortable—homes; children with night-terrors, and all sorts of wayward reactions; intellectuals, esthetes; delicate and refined invalids who are evasive and tyrannical with manifold symptoms and transitory dramatic episodes—it also includes patients delirious with fever, or reduced by a great variety of organic diseases; patients frozen with melancholy or indulging in an orgy of exuberant activity; patients living in a fantastic world with morbid visions and communications and uncanny influences, in whose universe one sees no coherence or logical structure; patients keenly logical and argumentative but embittered and seeing around them a hostile world with which they refuse to compromise."

At one time or another there are few of us who do not justify inclusion somewhere in this list, but if or when we do, it does not necessarily mean we are insane. Nor does it mean that merely because our difficulty in adjusting to life bears the label of "mental" or "psychiatric," we should be stigmatized. It is a curious commentary on human nature that in this day and generation it is eminently respectable to have a "nervous breakdown" but that the label "psychoneurosis" automatically relegates its owner into a group of crazy people.

Let us discard, then, our fear of the word "mental" or "psychiatric" and try to see the man or woman who is ill with one of these conditions as not different fundamentally from ourselves. Nor let us assume that "once insane, always insane" and consequently look with secret distrust on a recovered patient for an outbreak of renewed symptoms. As a matter of fact, many people do recover from psychiatric disabilities, even from the severe ones, the so-called "insanities." In any modern and well-conducted mental hospital up to as many as forty-five out of every one hundred patients who are admitted during the course of a year are discharged as cured within a year. Most of these persons resume their family and business lives as efficiently as before, and for all practical purposes no one would know that they had ever been mentally sick. To be sure, some are permitted by their families to come to the hospital only when their illness has reached such an advanced stage that reversal of their condition is improbable, and these are likely to remain.

The same thing is true with regard to certain physical illnesses. The earlier any condition of sickness is recognized and the earlier that proper treatment is invoked, the more likely are the chances of cure. A patient who is brought to a hospital for the first time when he is suffering from the final stages of tuberculosis or of cancer is apt to be incurable, and the best that can be hoped for is to make his declining days as comfortable as possible.

New methods of treatment are performing wonders for psychiatric conditions, and the percentage of recoveries is rising steadily as scientific knowledge of these conditions progresses. Indeed, today it is oftener easier to cure some of the troublesome and even crippling conditions of psychoneurosis than it is to effect a cure for rheumatism or high blood pressure. A hopeless attitude, therefore, toward most psychiatric disorders is not justified any more than is the stigma with which so many of these are surrounded.

With this background we are now ready to discuss how a psychiatric disability affects the discharged or returned serviceman. In the first place, suppose for the sake of clarity we attempt to draw up a rough classification of the more common psychiatric disorders that discharged soldiers may bring back with them. While neither complete nor scientifically quite accurate, the following will do for our purpose. In the order of their severity we can divide them into six groups.

Group I. The insanities or psychoses, as they are called officially. As stated previously, these are comparatively few in number, and, since most of them will require care in mental hospitals, they are not apt to be much of an immediate community problem of readjustment on their return.

Group II. The feeble-minded (called the *mentally defective*). These are men whose intelligence has failed to develop in average fashion. They are neither insane nor psychoneurotic but are defective from birth or early life in one of their basic articles of adjusting equipment, namely, their intelligence. Few will require institutional care on their return home, but their limitations of smartness, judgment, etc., should be recognized and care taken to ensure that they are not called upon for more in the way of responsibility and of work and family adjustment than they are equipped to give. They need a long-time protected and relatively pressureless environment, since their difficulty is caused by a *defect* that is irreversible rather than by an illness of a previously sound structure.

Group III. The psychopathic personalities. These persons are not insane, nor are they feeble-minded. They are apt, however, to be continuously antisocial in their behavior, and their difficulty would seem to lie in some deep-seated distortion of character that is seldom successfully treatable by any means yet known. Their family and community adjustment is likely to be stormy and often criminal.

Group IV. Structural diseases of the nervous system. These include men who display physical or mental symptoms (or both) as a result of damage to the brain or other portions of the nervous system. The damage may have been caused by disease, such as syphilis of the central nervous system, or it may have been produced by injury, such as a fractured skull or concussion. Not a few persons suffering from head injury, for example, whether obtained in combat or in an accident, undergo various changes in personality that may affect their community adjustment to a greater or lesser extent.

Most returned servicemen with some damage to the physical structure of a part of their nervous system will require active medical treatment, but the majority probably will not be in need of institutional care and can be treated at home or in their physician's office. In some cases the personality or emotional symptoms will persist long after all signs of external physical damage have disappeared, and these may gradually shade off into a chronic type of disorder in which the symptoms arrange themselves into certain constellations (groups of symptoms), to which the term "post-traumatic syndrome" is given.

Epilepsy probably should be included in this classification of structural diseases of the nervous system, although, strictly speaking, there are many cases of epilepsy in which no damage of any kind can be discovered in the brain or central nervous system. "Epilepsy" is a word used to designate certain types of convulsions or fits. A convulsive seizure can be caused by any one of a number of different reasons, of which physical damage to the brain is only one. A brain tumor can cause an epileptic seizure, and so can some kinds of gunshot wounds or other injuries to the skull. Perhaps a majority of convulsive seizures labeled "epilepsy" come from admittedly unknown causes (so-called "idiopathic" epilepsy).

Unless the seizures are very severe and very frequent, or unless they are accompanied by profound and sweeping changes in personality that produce antisocial behavior, most returning servicemen suffering from this malady will not require institutional care. They will, however, require very careful vocational placement in jobs specially chosen to avoid the danger of falling during a seizure and becoming tangled up in machinery or of becoming injured in some other fashion during an interval of unconsciousness. Given such protection and understanding, many—perhaps even most—servicemen suffering from epilepsy can be helped to lead useful and satisfying lives.

The outlook for cure depends on many factors, including the cause of any given case. In general, the treatment of epilepsy is the treatment of its cause. But even in those cases where the precise cause is unknown (the idiopathic types) much is being done these days in controlling the frequency and intensity of the seizures. Moreover, not a few cases clear up spontaneously as time goes on, although no one knows why. The families of servicemen with a diagnosis of epilepsy should not take a hopeless attitude toward the patient, since medical science is constantly adding to its understanding of this condition and, therefore, constantly improving its methods of treatment.

Group V. The combat fatigue disorders. These are emotional disorders characterized principally by various displays of anxiety or confusion or depression *that occur in basically normal and stable persons.* Mention was made earlier of some battle conditions so overpoweringly horrible that no human being could be expected to stand up under them without eventual breakdown. Prolonged thirst, hunger, exposure to cold or humid heat, lack of sleep, the need for taut nerves to be incessantly on the alert twenty-four hours a day, for days on end, with death lurking behind each tree or boulder—the accumulated impact of these things can and does wear down the strongest adjustment equipment. When this happens nerves go; previously sturdy and stable personalities break down and perhaps cry like babies, scream, or pull blankets over their heads, temporarily lose their memory, or lapse into lethargy or states of comalike depression.

Fortunately, most of these instances of combat fatigue recover from their acute manifestations fairly quickly, especially if psychiatric first-aid facilities are available, and a surprising number are returned to duty; either a resumption of combat duty or other duties in less exposed areas. The miracles of sulfa drugs, plasma, and first-aid battle dressings in keeping down the numbers of deaths from combat wounds have been one of the spectacular phenomena of World War II. If less publicized and less spectacular, the success with which military psychiatrists prevent cases of combat fatigue from becoming chronic disabilities through immediate and active treatment is equally miraculous. Some cases, to be sure, respond sluggishly and require evacuation to the States for more extensive treatment than can be given overseas. Most, however, as just stated are restored to duty of some kind within an astonishingly short space of time.

In World War I many of the psychiatric conditions that are now called "combat fatigue" were designated as "shell shock." That term was abandoned since it was discovered that only a small percentage of the men suffering from this kind of reaction had ever been exposed to shell fire. Indeed, there were more such cases among troops who had never left their training camps on this side than among those overseas. Furthermore, "shell shock" was a catch-all term into which was dumped almost any and every kind of psychiatric condition that occurred in a military setting. It was used indiscriminately, on the one hand to designate psychoneurotic reactions in servicemen who had been unstable for years prior to entering the army and who broke down within a few weeks of service, and on the other to describe the acute anxiety terrors of men in actual battle. For a time after the close of the last war "shell shock" achieved a sort of honorary distinction somewhat akin to that which now surrounds the term "nervous breakdown" when applied to a civilian.

In World War II military authorities are making a more sensible differentiation between various types of psychiatric conditions as seen among soldiers and sailors, with the result that "combat fatigue" is reserved to describe a special emotional disorder occurring only among men who fulfill two requirements: (1) the man must have been emotionally sound prior to the onset of his disorder, with no latent predisposition toward instability in his previous life history, and (2) his condition of combat fatigue must have arisen in a setting of actual battle or shortly thereafter.

Group VI. *The psychoneurotic.* The overwhelming majority of servicemen returning home with a psychiatric disability come within this category, which in turn can be broken down into several subdivisions. It is, indeed, a loosely used term but includes those suffering with anxiety states, either acute or chronic; those with psychosomatic disorders (functional conditions that reproduce symptoms suggestive of disease of some physical organ without that organ's actually being damaged); those with obsessive thoughts or compulsive actions; and those with numerous fears and phobias.

Unlike the soldier who develops a combat-fatigue disorder as described in Group V above, the ex-serviceman returning home with a psychoneurosis is likely to have been predisposed to emotional instability long before he entered military service. This is not invariably true, but some previously unsuspected and latent predisposition has been found in such large numbers of men discharged with a diagnosis of psychoneurosis that up to July, 1944, military authorities have regarded only 20 per cent of this group's disabilities as being entirely caused by their military duties.

While anxiety states represent one of the major subdivisions of psychoneurosis, yet any psychoneurotic condition can be—and often is—accompanied by some manifestation of anxiety. Anxiety, that vague uncomfortable feeling that something unpleasant is hanging over our heads without our being able to say just what it is, is probably present in dilute form in us all at any given moment. Its origins are none too well known, but some psychiatrists are inclined to believe it stems from our feelings of hatred and aggressiveness that are aroused whenever we are frustrated in some of our desires. Since everyone is frustrated in something or other many times each day, anxiety in at least mild form is likely to be ever-present. Ordinarily, we drain off our trivial anxieties by overcoming our frustrations or by philosophically accepting them, and the anxiety is dispelled without markedly affecting our adjustment.

Once in a while, however, we reach a point where pressure, frustration, or deprivation becomes so strong that it cannot be tolerated. On such occasions we may react with inner feelings of hatred and aggressiveness so violent that they frighten us when we intuitively sense what might happen by way of retaliation if we turned that aggressiveness outward against those persons or things that frustrate us. Therefore, since we are civilized and God-fearing people, the very intensity of our hatred creates anxiety, which comes from expectation of punishment for toying with the temptation to loosen the inhibitions that help us maintain our standards of personal and social acceptability. As a consequence, instead of directing our aggressive feelings outward against others, we turn them inward destructively against ourselves. Thus are produced associated feelings of guilt, of depression, and of tension.

Anxiety may appear in acute form in such stark, unmistakable terms as terror or even panic, but by the time a serviceman returns home after being discharged for some psychiatric condition, which perhaps is characterized by anxiety, the acute manifestations likely have subsided into chronic ones. Nevertheless, under the spur of renewed pressures arising out of attempts to make a civilian adjustment, and out of renewed frustrations or deprivations of psychological needs; chronic anxiety is capable of flaring up once more into acute displays. So-called "startle reactions" over sudden noises or sudden movements are one example of such flare-ups.

One of the most troublesome ways in which anxiety may select (unconsciously, of course) to make itself known is through some psychosomatic condition: *i.e.*, through some set of physical symptoms. Returned servicemen who express their anxiety in this way, as a result of the difficulties of adjusting to the frustrations of civilian living, are apt to be impatiently called "hypochondriacs" and to be accused of suffering from imaginary illness.

Actually, their illness is not imaginary; on the contrary, it is very real and very painful, and they are genuinely miserable, but it is an illness of the man's *feelings* and not one of the particular organ of the body that appears to be affected. For example, Joe is discharged from the service with a diagnosis of "Psychoneurosis—anxiety—referable to heart" because military life caused him to complain of weakness on exertion, palpitation of his heart, shortness of breath, and pains in his chest. These symptoms often are found in people who have actual valvular disease of the heart or whose cardiac muscles are physically damaged, but they can be found also in others whose hearts have been examined repeatedly by competent specialists and declared sound and in excellent condition. How, then, explain Joe's heart symptoms?

If Joe's heart symptoms happen to be an expression of anxiety they might be explained in this way: If Joe was in New Guinea and unexpectedly encountered a Jap slithering toward him in the grass of the jungle with rifle pointed at him, Joe would, of course, be afraid. Any of us would. As a result of his quite understandable fear Joe's heart would probably begin to pound and beat rapidly (palpitate); he would grow pale and breathless; his insides would constrict and tie themselves into knots; and he would feel weak. In other words, Joe would feel or show many of the normal manifestations of fear. Despite the fact, however, that many of these manifestations involved functions of his heart, Joe's heart as an organ of his body was still as sound and husky as it was before he met the Jap. It was merely the way his heart *operated* that produced the symptoms, and when he had safely finished off the Jap they disappeared.

But perhaps the particular Joe in whom we are interested had never been in New Guinea and had never met a Jap. Perhaps he never got further in military life than a few months in a training camp in Tennessee or Georgia or Virginia. Nothing of an especially acute nature had occurred in camp to frighten him; nevertheless he, too, developed many symptoms that at least outwardly resembled symptoms of the heart disease that Joe in New Guinea had. In this case perhaps our Joe was just naturally unsuited to military life. Perhaps he was one of those immature personalities, discussed in a previous chapter, whose need to be protected, fussed over, and taken care of by a doting mother was so great that it was frustrated by the impersonal life of the army, that he could no longer face the responsibility of functioning on his own, and that he felt progressively more insecure.

As a result of these feelings Joe grew apprehensive, only instead of developing into fear, his feelings about it all fell into that category of apprehensiveness called "anxiety." It wasn't a Jap sniper who caused it, but his own inner lack of emotional maturity. So, because he was anxious, Joe's heart began to act like the heart of anyone frightened by some more tangible, physical danger; it beat rapidly, it caused shortness of breath, it made him feel weak, and it gave him pains in his chest. *But his physical heart organ remained sound.* This is what Joe found it hard to believe no matter how many doctors tried to reassure him.

"If my symptoms are referable to my heart," Joe figured, "it stands to reason that my heart must be affected." So long as the frustration of his need to be protected by his mother continued, his symptoms of "heart" disease (*i.e.*, his anxiety) continued likewise. Of course, Joe's reasoning was faulty, but until he could be helped to mature so that he could stand on his own feet without maternal support or, if his immaturity was too great for this, until he was restored to his mother's bosom, Joe's heart symptoms could not be expected to subside. Joe was suffering from one of the psychoneuroses which is termed a "psychosomatic disorder": *i.e.*, his feelings affected the functioning of an organ of his body to an extent that made him unsuitable for military service.

In doing this Joe must not be thought of as a malingerer or "gold-bricker." He definitely did not fake his symptoms in order to get out of the army. The mechanisms that produced Joe's heart symptoms operated in the unconscious part of his mind, and he was honestly both unaware of and puzzled by their results. It would be both cruel and unfair to accuse him of deliberately manufacturing his disability out of whole cloth. His illness was not imaginary, and the discomfort he felt from his symptoms was very genuine. Consequently, he should be treated like any other sick person in whom the discovery of the causes of his sickness and the treatment of these causes, rather than treatment merely of the symptoms, become the scientific way of going about restoration to health.

Not all emotional disorders are destructive in their effects. Sometimes they are the reason why a person becomes a great painter or musician or humanitarian, and sometimes psychiatrists deliberately refrain from advising treatment of them on the basis that "to cure a neurosis might spoil a poet." Dr. George S. Stevenson, Medical Director of the National Committee for Mental Hygiene, makes this interesting comment about the positive and negative value of a psychoneurosis:

"I am very anxious that in any public interpretation of the neurosis that the negative aspects of this condition be balanced with an appreciation of the fact that it frequently has its positive side. It is a form of personality development, characterized by special focalized sensitivity and reactivity. Sometimes this sensitivity may be so keen as to completely incapacitate the person. More frequently, however, he is only partially handicapped by it and in some respects, and often at the same time, it may be a positive asset and may be the basis of a talent that is responsible for his social contribution and personal satisfaction.

"I recently encountered an instance in which this appeared quite clearly in a man who had been discharged from the service. This man had worked for 12 years in a position almost devoid of contact with human beings. He disliked his job and wanted to be rid of it, but showed his maturity by deciding to hold on to it until he had prepared himself for something better. This man had a specially focalized sensitivity to the life problems of people and it is understandable that his job gave him little satisfaction because it touched upon this sensitivity so little. It is significant that he used his spare time to prepare himself for the field of social work at a nearby university. In the midst of this professional training he was drafted and in the latter part of basic training had to be discharged for psychoneurosis. He became terribly upset about rifle practice where a special point was made of focusing each shot on a Jap or a German. He lost sleep, ate poorly and became so unable to function that discharge was inescapable. The social work was the positive expression of his sensitivity. The rifle practice and its effects were the negative. After discharge he returned to his job, resumed his training and with one exception seemed to be functioning at his pre-service level. The exception was that he had a piece of paper with the word 'psychoneurosis' on it and that worried him. In discussing the matter with him it became evident to him that to lose the sensitivity that had broken him down in the army, if it could be accomplished would mean to lose the interest in social work out of which he hoped to derive both satisfaction and social contribution. He chose to retain his 'neurosis.' "

The particular serviceman in whom we are interested may be one of the hundreds of thousands who return home before the ending of the war by reason of a discharge for psychiatric disability. If so, we do not need to be unduly disturbed. We can learn to understand the meaning of his various types of reactions and respond toward him accordingly; we can refuse to be awed or frightened by their seeming mysteriousness or by their illogical nature; we can take the sensible attitude that his actions are merely intensifications of our own, given similar provocation; and we can oppose vigorously any stigma cast upon him because his trouble is psychiatric. Most of all, we can realize that in most cases the outlook for an adjustment to civilian life that will prove as satisfactory to him as to us is excellent; that modern methods of psychiatric treatment are performing wonders; and, finally, that the kind of atmosphere we create at home for him will do more than anything else to expedite his recovery.

6

THE FIRST WEEKS AT HOME

HOME again!—whether demobilized at the end of the war or discharged earlier for some disability—it's a grand and glorious feeling. No more reveille at crack of dawn; no more jumping to attention for every bombastic second lieutenant; no more cowering in the slime of a foxhole watching to see where a Big One will hit.

Corp. Russell J. Richards is one of those returned soldiers who happens to be articulate about his feelings on coming home. His are the typical reactions of most men who have been away any length of time and who now find themselves back in their home towns. Corporal Richards tells, for example, of how visions of his mother's cooking, of hot baths in a real bathtub, and of automobile trips with his girl were about his only supports for flagging morale when things got too tough at the front. He describes how he idealized and dreamed of the hundred and one sorely missed little details of everyday civilian life and his joy in planning those first few weeks at home. He recalls ruefully how at that time he scoffed at talk about the difficulties to be faced in adjusting to home life again, how he felt confident that adjustment would be no problem at all for him, and how he would merely have to start right in where he left off on entering the army—hunt up his old friends, buy a new suit of civilian clothes, and in general resume living just as if he had never been away. Adjustment? That was all high-brow talk.

And some of it did come true, Corporal Richards remembers. His mother's cooking was just as good as ever, the delights of a tub bath were fully up to expectations, and his girl seemed genuinely—if a bit demurely—glad to see him again. Even his father gave respectful ear to tales of derring-do, and it all seemed at first very gratifying and very much as he had pictured it. But Corporal Richards, who is one of those rare people who are able to laugh good-naturedly at themselves and who can put their feelings into words, now admits that it wasn't long before flaws began to appear and the horrid doubt flashed across his mind that maybe there was something to this adjustment business that he hadn't counted on. For one thing, he discovered that, cordial as his girl was, she had been plunged, by his return, into a conflict of loyalties with friends she had made while he was away. For another, he found it incredible to realize that the girl had gotten a job and wasn't always free to run at his every beck and call. In looking back on it now Corporal Richards chuckles in amused exasperation at the idealized image he had nurtured while he was away.

Corporal Richards experienced other disillusionments. The old crowd he had planned on rejoining on his return had mostly evaporated. Some were still in service, while others had been discharged and moved to other towns. Disconsolately, he drifted down to Nick's diner, where he had been in the habit of sitting on a stool, with elbows on the counter, and arguing long into the evening with Nick over a cup of coffee. But now Nick was too busy serving a horde of war workers to do more than give him a friendly wave of welcome as he bustled from kitchen to counter with laden trays. Now several months after his return Corporal Richards can see that he began to grow grumpy and irritable from all this disillusionment. Things in the home town weren't really at all what he had expected them to be, and he reverted to a practice common to most of us under similar circumstances: *i.e.*, he projected his feelings of irritability onto others, instead of acknowledging that the trouble lay within himself. "What's the matter with everyone, anyway?" he asked himself. "Why can't things stay like they used to be? Why must everything be different? Heck, back in the army there were some things at least that a fellow could depend on."

The climax was reached when a hastily planned trip to the lake with his girl had to be abandoned through lack of coupons for gasoline and the refusal of the man at the service station to sell him any without coupons. Corporal Richards says he really blew up then. Did the man mean that a veteran with two years' overseas service and a string of ribbons across his chest didn't rate any privileges? Gas coupons? Those are for civilians. What kind of a country is this, anyway? Maybe the old foxhole wasn't so bad, after all. At least, over on the other side no one had ever asked him for coupons to gas up his mud-stained jeep before setting out on a reconnaissance trip—and so, on and on.

SOLDIER TO CIVILIAN

Corporal Richards is only one returned soldier, but tens of thousands of his buddies feel as he did, bitter, bewildered, and disillusioned over the realities of homecoming. Nothing turns out quite as they expected and they quickly find that the difficulties of adjustment on going into military life are no whit more painful than those experienced on coming out. Moreover, the adjustment difficulties on returning home affect not only the soldier himself but his family and friends as well, and the realization that his reactions are hurting them adds to his pain. He recognizes that some of his behavior is difficult, but he is likely not to understand why he feels and acts as he does and he is thoroughly miserable and sometimes ashamed and guilty. We, then, his family and friends, must do our best to understand, even if he can't, and out of our understanding develop attitudes that will help shorten his period of adjustment.

In order to do this suppose we try to break down some of these adjustment difficulties, first, into those facing *all* returned servicemen, whether demobilized or discharged, and, second, into those special adjustment difficulties confronting men who have been given a medical discharge for physical or psychiatric reasons and who consequently return home before the war is over.

No matter what the reasons for separation from military service, virtually all returned soldiers begin to experience a mixture of feelings after the excitement of the first few days at home has subsided. Relief at leaving the army is mixed with an illogical resentment at having to do so, and happiness at being home again is mingled with sadness over leaving the boys of Company K. Out of this mixture of feelings may gradually be distilled an attitude of mild depression, which, while probably temporary, is uncomfortable while it lasts. It is compounded chiefly out of a realization of the loss of group support. Attention was drawn in an earlier chapter to the strenuous efforts made by military officials to instill a feeling of group loyalty and identification among servicemen; to cause them to feel that they were an indispensable part of their group and that they in turn could depend on the group. By and large, these efforts succeeded, sometimes only too well. Month after month in the army the man in whom we are interested identified himself with the group imperceptibly but closer and closer until it became a very part of him and he felt helpless and insecure without its invisible support.

True enough, he griped and grumbled, as does every good soldier, about his officers, his buddies, and the regulations, but deep down within him he sensed his dependency on the group and developed a powerful loyalty. In this respect his grumbling was the same kind that is seen in a husband and wife, whose mutual bickerings conceal a basic affection so deep that they will resist separation and fly fiercely to the defense of each other if attacked.

But now the group is broken up; our soldier has been transformed into an ex-serviceman; he is on his own, and only part of him likes it. What about the future? With what new groups can he identify himself and thus derive continuing group support? To what or to whom can he attach the loyalties he felt for his group? Where will he find security and thus lessen some of the anxiety that assails him? He may not phrase his problems in just these words, but these are some of the difficulties for which he must find solutions before his civilian adjustment becomes satisfactory.

He makes pathetic attempts to bring some order into his

chaotic feelings. For one thing [and this is strange], he discovers he has forgotten how to discipline himself. In the army he became a creature of routine dependent on army regulations and a sergeant's orders for almost every breath he took. It had been hard at first, but gradually he accepted this routinization of his life and even found it easier to follow orders blindly than to think for himself. Months or years in the service caused him to forget how to make many everyday decisions for himself, and now that he is at home and functioning no longer in an orderly and regimented environment he feels ill at ease.

An understanding of this will go far to help his family to be patient with his indecisions and doubts, which he may show in the most trivial ways, as well as in some important ones. For example, he literally may not know how to organize or what to do with his time those first few weeks, with no one to direct him.

He putters aimlessly around the house, starts off to a picnic, changes his mind and decides he'd rather go to a movie, and wonders if today or tomorrow would be better for mowing the lawn. He drives his mother frantic by sometimes asking over and over if dinner isn't ready and at other times being naïvely surprised that he is an hour late. On the other hand, out of his need to avoid making his own decisions or having to do too much thinking for himself he may try desperately to institute at home a replica of his military habits, where everything is done at precisely the same time and always in the same way. This brings further exasperation to his bewildered family, especially if they have been easygoing, without too much concern for meticulous living. He insists—banteringly, perhaps, but nonetheless with steely determination—that if supper is set for six o'clock, then the family must be at the table with forks upraised as the clock strikes, or maybe that his sister's happy-go-lucky habit of stowing the dishpan under the sink at one time and on the cupboard shelf the next calls for rebuke, or that his young brother's pajamas and ties must be hung neatly on closet hooks instead of being left scattered helter-skelter all around the room.

Before entering the army our man may have been equally careless, and the family does not know what to make of the change that has occurred in him. Everything, he insists, should be reduced to a system, "the army system"; it makes things easier that way, he says. Maybe it does, the family grudgingly concedes, but it also takes a lot of the fun out of living, and they shake their collective heads despairingly over the conflict between their desire to make things pleasant for the returned soldier and their exasperation over the disarrangement of *their* mode of living.

Learning to take responsibility for one's own management and the need for making one's own decisions come hard after a prolonged period when these things were all done for one by others, but bit by bit the returned soldiers (most of them, at any rate) do take over the job of organizing their own lives, and this problem eventually disappears.

Another problem that besets, secretly perhaps, almost all returned servicemen is fear of the future. Many of them appear outwardly cocky and confident; but inwardly they wonder about their ability to get established in civilian life. Even though they may know they can have the old job back for the asking, they raise all sorts of doubts within themselves about its stability, its likelihood for promotion, whether their absence for so long has gotten them out of the swing of the old job, etc. They are reassured perhaps by governmental promises to take care of the veterans, but at the same time they wonder about their place in the postwar world and how the shape of things to come will affect them.

If they return unmarried they permit doubts to creep in over their ability to support a wife and to make a good husband. If they had just begun college when they entered service, they wonder, is it really wise to spend another three or four years in a belated attempt to complete their education?

This fear of the future is based partly on realistic apprehensions, but partly it is apt to be a displacement of anxiety about their adequacy to function on their own after the dependency that military existence threw about them is withdrawn.

Closely allied to the returned soldier's fear of the future may be an attitude of timidity or shyness or of self-conscious silence when in a group of civilians. This, too, may perplex his family, for prior to going away he may have been the life of the party. Such an attitude can mean several different things. It may mean, for example, that he has been out of the current of civilian interests and activities for so long that he really does not know what is going on. Magazines and home-town papers may have reached him infrequently, and letters may not have kept him up to date with regard to local happenings. Besides, he was often too occupied with military duties to do much reading. Consequently, he finds he hasn't much to talk about with civilians. He hasn't heard the local gossip discussed eagerly by the home folks; he hasn't kept up with the political situation, either local or national; he can't even answer questions intelligently about the strategy of the Supreme Allied Command in the Normandy campaign, since all he saw of it was the infinitesimally tiny segment in which he personally was engaged. All in all, he feels like a "wash-out" and he senses with a renewed despair the gulf that sets him apart from those he longs to join.

A problem that exerts almost immediate influence on his civilian adjustment, on his family relationships, social relationships, and general community relationships, is that of suitable control of the aggressiveness he as a soldier was taught to develop. Aggressiveness in a soldier fighting a war is a military virtue, but the same aggressiveness expressed in a civilian milieu may be regarded by others as a vice. This shift in values is hard for some returned men to understand. Moreover, it is far easier to unleash aggression than it is to retame it. Some returned servicemen are going to fail to restrain their aggressiveness once they leave the army and will get into trouble with the civilian authorities. Among them will be a proportion of the psychopathic personalities described in Chap. 5. Others will come to make this adjustment satisfactorily but perhaps only after one or more unpleasant experiences.

Such aggressiveness does not necessarily have to be expressed in physical violence. Too blunt, brusque speech; a domineering, belligerent manner that offends; curt commands to others—these, too, may retard the personal as well as the vocational adjustment of many men unless they can substitute more diplomatic ways for getting along with people. Parents, wives, and friends may be distressed at such shows of pugnacity and at the rebuffs in civilian life they produce.

Gradually, however, most of the men who display such attitudes will be enabled to drain off their aggressive feelings

· 121 ·

or at least turn them into socially acceptable channels, through the same means used by the rest of us whose aggressiveness perhaps is less intense: namely, through competitive sports, through music or the other arts, through the give-and-take of social intercourse, and through directing it into our jobs.

An annoyance that is trivial, although painful to the family, is likely to occur in the vulgarity of the ex-soldier's language. Military life is a rough-and-ready existence; niceties of speech are exchanged for utilitarianism, and humor is apt to be of the latrine variety. Oaths and profanities become commonplace so that they are used automatically and unnoticed. They soon lose all meaning—if they ever possessed any to begin with—and, in common with a majority of his military friends, the man with whose civilian adjustment we are concerned will probably come home with a vocabulary interlarded with new expressions that will shock his mother. If so, she need not be alarmed. In time it will pass, the more quickly if scant attention is paid it, as he begins gradually to want to make himself more similar to those around him at home: *i.e.*, as he forms new identifications, this time with civilian rather than military groups.

In the same way, much of the ex-serviceman's conversation is likely to revolve around the subject of women and sex, particularly when he turns raconteur. Soldiers of course have been women-starved for months or years; most of them are in the lusty period of adolescence or post-adolescence, when biologic urges are normal but powerful, and it is only natural that at times their thoughts should turn to sex. This is the more likely because, in their exclusively masculine military environment, they were deprived of the usual civilian opportunities for draining off sex feelings through wholesome recreational contacts with girls, and as a result they have come to overvalue this biologic instinct. War, of course, is an elemental struggle, and almost everything associated with it tends to become reduced to primitive forms of expression. Sex is no exception, and under the life and death exigencies of warfare it, too, is apt to lose many of its civilian sublimations and refinements.

If the ex-soldier's stories seem to be pretty salty don't take them too seriously. Part of his motive for telling them may be nothing but the carry-over of military habit, another part may be due to his inner uncertainty of himself, which makes it necessary for him to pose as a sophisticated man about town, while yet a third part of his motive may come from the mischievous little-boy desire to draw attention to himself by shocking the old folks. Ignore his sexy stories or tactfully change the subject and it won't be long before he forgets them.

All returned soldiers pass through a period of disillusionment as an inescapable part of their total problem of civilian adjustment. They become disillusioned about their home town, about their jobs, about their freedom from military restrictions, but most of all about their families and friends. This last disillusionment is hardest of all to adapt to because of the feelings of guilt it engenders. Even the soldier who was so self-centered or immature that he never felt any deep attachment to his home town, his job, or his family builds up an artificial idolization of these by a process of imitating the genuine nostalgia of more mature buddies. Army songs, army propaganda, army customs all combine to produce a pattern of eulogy of home life that exerts a powerfully suggestive effect on many men. Because they are expected to be home-sick and because they are expected to dwell everlastingly on the good old days in the good old town of X, and of good old Mom and Pop, and kid sister Sue and brother Tom (to say nothing of good old Dotty, the girl friend), they build up a picture of home life that is Utopia itself.

With most of them the process is a genuine one, but among those whose verbalized idealization of home life is the most vociferous are to be found a proportion of emotionally immature men of all ages, whose home-town sentimentality is akin to the maudlin tears elicited by a "mammy" song. It is among this latter group that the impact of disillusionment strikes the hardest. Because their idealization was so largely fictitious in the first place, the resulting let-down feeling is interpreted by them as a personal betrayal, and the more artificial the original build-up, the more bitter their indignation and denunciation that the folks at home are not the paragons of perfection they expected them to be.

A period of disillusionment is inevitable for all returned soldiers, immature or not, before their concept of themselves finally is transformed from a military into a civilian one, and out of their disillusionment emerges a variety of attitudes and displays of behavior that may hurt and perplex the family. While they were away they had put out of their minds the multitude of petty but inescapable irritations of civilian living and remembered only the pleasant things.

Private Frank Mullins, discharged from an infantry regiment in Italy because of severe arthritis in his leg, found, for example, that he completely dissociated from his thinking his mother's annoying prewar habit of asking where he was going and what time he would be home; his father's usurpation of the bathroom for a leisurely shave when he was himself rushing to get cleaned up for a date; the blaring of the radio at the neighbor's next door on a Sunday morning when he wanted to sleep; or the way his girl friend invariably made him wait while she gave interminable last-minute touches to her hair before coming downstairs. These irritations, which had made him unhappy at times before he entered the army, were all forgotten when he visualized home from the beach at Anzio. But now home had become a reality once more and after the first few days Private Mullins was disturbed to find himself seeing flaws in its fancied perfections. True, during those first few days it was just as he had pictured it. His father and mother acted as if Frank was an honored guest—and that, in a sense, was exactly what he was—a guest. Part of him reveled in his family's solicitous ministrations, which seemed to realize his overseas anticipations. But another, deeper part was vaguely uneasy at their considerations. It seemed almost unnatural, as if it were too good to last.

About the fourth or fifth day the novelty of Private Mullins' homecoming began to wear off. His family resumed their everyday habits, many of which irritated him. While in the army, often overcome by homesickness, he had minimized these or completely forgotten them. Now he faced the irritations and pinpricks of everyday life, back in full force. Private Mullins was conflicted about all the problems mentioned a few pages back in connection with leaving the army, but perhaps he didn't see them as clearly as we have. All he knew was that he felt strange and puzzled and hurt and a bit melancholy. Something had to account for his feelings, and, since he wasn't aware of the real causes for them (*i.e.*, his missing all the things that military life had come to mean for him), he was required to pin the responsibility onto something concrete. What more plausible, therefore, than to make the annoyances of civilian living the scapegoat? So Private Mullins, as well as all the other returned servicemen of whom he is a prototype, may express his discontent with himself through taking it out on others, especially on those with whom he comes in closest and most frequent contact.

Thus, he grows moody and restless. To his own as well as to the family's astonishment (for by a reverse process, they had forgotten all *his* irritating habits and had come to idealize *him* while he was away) he becomes snappish or impatient. He finds fault and complains. His speech is sarcastic at one time and sullen at another. He develops an argumentative streak that may grow so heated as to arouse suspicion that he is deliberately trying to provoke a quarrel. The family is unhappy and so is he. He still doesn't realize that his dissatisfaction lies chiefly within himself rather than with others, and he is convinced that they don't understand him. Indeed, he may go so far in his bitterness as to believe these others take enjoyment in making him irritated, and a mild persecutory feeling may develop. What to do? Where to go to find people who will understand him?

Private Mullins doesn't have to ponder these questions long before the answer suggests itself. If these civilians don't understand him, even members of his own family, he can seek out other ex-soldiers who do. And so he drops in at the Legion rooms or those of some other veterans' organization and at once feels at home. Here he finds an atmosphere savoring of his former Company K. Here are other bewildered and disillusioned lost souls like himself, huddling together for a pitiful retention of the group support they came to lean on in the army. Here are people who speak his language, and here are those who commiserate comprehendingly with him in his distress. At the Legion they all can gripe about civilian life just as they did about KP duty in the army, and without hurting the feelings of those they love; they can curse meaninglessly without causing raised eyebrows; they can reminisce interminably as they endeavor to project themselves back into the environment where they felt understood and secure and confident. Once more they recapture at least the ghost of the feeling of support they once derived from identification with the group, and for the moment their civilian irritations vanish.

Veterans' organizations come into existence to meet these needs of Private Mullins and his millions of former buddies. For a time after returning home these needs are healthy and legitimate. In months or in a year or two most ex-servicemen, however, have completed their adjustment to civilian life. They have become full-fledged civilians again, and their need to perpetuate their former military existence grows less desperate. This group (which constitutes a majority of all returned soldiers) gains sufficient security from their adjustment to life in the community to permit them to loosen their dependency on the veterans' organization. They drop in at the clubhouse once in a while, to be sure, for they enjoy quite normally the opportunity to meet old friends and to keep in touch with new developments, but for the most part the veterans' organization for this group (which, to repeat, represents the majority) becomes in time merely a pleasant club to be used only when the spirit moves.

For a minority, however, the situation is different. For the immature, the emotionally unstable, or the dependency-conditioned ex-serviceman, or for the returned soldier whose personality is too rigid or perhaps too timid to allow him to adapt to the role of a civilian, the veterans' organization becomes the focal point around which much of his existence centers. His original need on returning from military life to find group support within its sanctuary does not—as in the case of the sturdier, more mature personality—grow less. On the contrary, as the discomforts of assuming civilian responsibility for his self-management mount in painfulness his attachment to the organization mounts similarly in intensity. In this respect he is not unlike the perpetual adolescent who, despite mature physical years and success in business, continues emotionally to live in his college atmosphere, who attends class reunions, litters his room with football trophies, covers his walls with class photographs, and, like as not, is the permanent class secretary.

This type of ex-soldier is at the clubhouse every minute he can spare and is among the die-hards who habitually have to be driven out late at night. He leans upon the favors granted by its officers or influential members. He debates noisily and at great length on trivial matters at business meetings. He searches indefatigably for new members, and his tenuous security brims over if he is elected to office. At its meetings he is vitriolic in his diatribes against the ranks of 4-F's, "slackers," conscientious objectors, and other noncombatants, into which he is inclined to relegate most civilians, and he introduces heated resolutions against them. "The organization first, all ex-servicemen who—sadly—have not joined it yet, second, and to hell with the rest of the world" is apt to be the working philosophy of this kind of fanatical veterans' organization member.

It is all understandable, even if it may contain implications for community as well as for national disquietude. The more immature or insecure or emotionally unstable a man is, the more trouble he has in identifying himself with the healthier bulk of the community. The more trouble he experiences in doing this, the more likely he is to limit his relationships only to those in whom he senses similarity. Veterans' organizations can and do perform valuable community services, to civilians and former soldiers alike. But it would be running counter to facts to deny that, if or when their control is seized by overaggressive individuals with a ruthless lust for power, when a segment of their membership causes them to become isolated from the main current of community harmony, or when their policies and practices encourage in many of their members an unhealthy dependency on the perpetuation of a phase of life that has long since passed, their influence is apt to be against the public good.

What has been written so far pertains to some of the problems of civilian adjustment of *all* returned soldiers. It will be well at this point if we look at some of the special adjustment problems of the soldier who is discharged before the end of the war because of some physical or psychiatric handicap. To this group should be added the million and a half others who were rejected at induction centers as unsuitable for military service, the so-called "4-F's." These combined groups experience many of the discomforts of adjustment that face demobilized servicemen and in some, additional ones arising out of the particular nature of their handicap.

The first few weeks at home for the soldier discharged because of some battle wound or deformity are apt to be agonizingly painful, not only for him but for his family and friends. Of course, the chances are that he will not be discharged from government hospitals until everything possible has been done to repair his injuries. When this has been accomplished, however, there will remain many with residual and visible impairments that affect their emotional attitudes and, consequently, their civilian adjustment. There is, for example, the ex-serviceman who returns home with an amputation or a marked limp or some other conspicuous limitation of motion of a limb or, perhaps worst of all, with a hideous disfigurement of the face that the most skilled plastic surgery cannot wholly eradicate. What problems of adjustment do these men face and what attitudes shall their families take to make that adjustment smoother? One of the most painful is their doubt of acceptance by the family. No matter how securely they felt entrenched in the love of parents or wife before the injury, they cannot wholly rid themselves of the horrid fear that perhaps these persons will now find them repulsive and that as a consequence their affections may cool. Such handicapped men may also feel this way about their first meeting with former friends and employers. So unsure are they of their reception that some may be seen searching the faces of loved ones as if to detect the signs of rejection they fear.

How to deal with this attitude in a returned soldier presents a difficult problem for the family. If—as should be the case—they have been informed before his return of the nature and degree of his injury, they can prepare themselves emotionally in advance to school their feelings when he walks into the house. If they have been given no preliminary information about his disability, however, the shock felt by the family at the first sight of his deformity may betray them, and if the deformity actually is repulsive they would be less than human if they failed to show how they feel. However, with the tension of the first meeting over, parents, wives, and others can do much through *their* attitudes to help during the difficult weeks of adjustment to follow. They can adopt a realistic manner that does not minimize the seriousness of the situation but on the other hand does not exaggerate it.

If a man returns with a missing arm or leg it will do no good to put on a bright, artificial Pollyanna manner that pretends to ignore it, nor will it help to dissolve into tears and absolve him from all attempts at self-help. Instead, the constructive attitude for the family to take is one of admitting the limitations on certain activities imposed by the handicap and then proceeding to help the man compensate for these limitations by searching for substitutes. To accomplish this families will need as never before to develop the qualities sometimes referred to as the "two I's," *i.e.*, Imagination and Ingenuity. They will need imagination in order to put themselves in his place and to sense how he feels about his handicap and its reaction on them. They will need ingenuity once this is done, in order to devise ways and means for compensating for the handicap. In almost all cases families can succeed in achieving this, but no specific blueprints are available and each instance will require the exercise of clever individual thinking.

Repeated reassurance that his handicap makes no difference in their affection for him also will help the physically disabled serviceman. To be effective this reassurance must be genuine. If a wife feels secretly a measure of true revulsion for the nature of her husband's deformity (especially if affection for him had been only lukewarm in the first place), then all her words to the contrary will fail to reassure. These men are extraordinarily sensitive to the impressions they create in others and they develop an uncanny sharpness in detecting feelings of rejection in others no matter how cleverly disguised. Reassurance can best be expressed through attitudes, not words. Develop an attitude, for example, that takes it for granted that the disabled man will resume the performance of every activity he formerly engaged in, except for those that involve the areas definitely limited by his handicap. Don't absolve him from all duties or responsibilities and, most of all, don't baby him.

If he was a mature, sturdy personality before his injury, he will resent being pitied and babied. If he was formerly immature and dependent, babying will only crystallize his self-pity into an eager and permanent loss of all incentive to become reliant. Give him tasks to perform around the house, scold him good-naturedly when he deserves it just as you used to do, encourage him to resume old friendships as if nothing had happened, let him feel from your attitude that you stand always four-square behind him, and, above all, *do not make him dependent.*

This admonition holds the most serious possible importance for the future of the individual disabled serviceman, as well as for the nation as a whole. As discussed in Chap. 2, the temptation to dependency, to be taken care of and absolved from adult responsibilities resides in us all. Most of us under ordinary circumstances reject that temptation and continue to extract satisfaction out of independence. But when circumstances occur out of the ordinary, when injury or sickness lowers our resistance to this temptation, or when we have failed to achieve emotional maturity, then it is easy to heed the "call of the cradle" and permit—or even demand —that we be taken care of.

A soldier discharged for some physical or psychiatric disability is entitled by a grateful nation to every last ounce of help he needs. But the help that he *needs* and the help that he *wants* do not always coincide.

Unpalatable as it may be to take, the impersonal fact stands out that a goodly number of ex-servicemen are going to want to be taken care of in far greater degree than their actual disabilities justify. World War I, with its two-thirds fewer men involved, is a sobering confirmation of this. Veterans Administration figures state that in June, 1920, a year and a half after the Armistice, there were 17,471 veterans remaining under hospital care. By June, 1942, these figures had jumped to 56,073 World War I veterans under hospital care under the Veterans Administration. Of these, 76 *per cent were nonservice-connected disabilities.* A breakdown of classifications revealed that 4,900 were tuberculosis cases; 16,514 were general medical cases; and 34,659 *were neuropsychiatric cases.* Careful studies of these men indicate that many had demanded hospitalization because they had given up the fight to become adjusted to civilian living and had surrendered to coddling by the government. Original disabilities that, under wiser management by families, by governmental agencies, and by veterans' organizations might have been reduced to fractional degrees, became total, and the veterans were encouraged to lean indefinitely on public substitutes for individual initiative and self-help.

This encouragement to continued dependency has, unfortunately, been strengthened by well-meaning but unwise governmental policies concerning methods of payment for military disabilities. Up to the present time for both World Wars I and II it has been the government's practice to pay a disabled veteran a monthly sum (depending on the degree of disability) every month as long as the disability lasts. Under such circumstances it is inevitable—human nature being what it is—that not a few dependency-conditioned veterans decide (at least unconsciously) that they cannot afford to get well, since in that case payments would cease. There is, of course, no question but what a disabled ex-serviceman is entitled to financial and other help when his disability was incurred while fighting for his country. But existing methods for discharging our national debt of gratitude to these men all too often do them a dis-service by inviting a prolongation of—or even rendering permanent—their period of ineffectiveness as productive members of the community.

It is encouraging, therefore, to note that this unhealthy situation recently has been given official recognition by Colonel William Menninger, chief of the psychiatric division of the Surgeon General's office of the Army Medical Corps. Colonel Menninger, with the endorsement of many other medical officers as well as civilian physicians, urges that disability payments be made on a *lump sum* basis, rather than spread out in monthly doles as long as the disability remains. Should this policy be adopted thousands of veterans who otherwise would be tempted to remain "disabled" indefinitely in order to be eligible to receive governmental support, will be encouraged to stand on their own feet and re-enter civilian life on an independent, self-respecting basis.

For his own sake as well as for that of our nation, let us help the disabled ex-serviceman to the fullest extent of his need; let us be sure that our aid is of the kind that helps him to help himself.

For the returned soldier who is discharged because of a psychiatric handicap the problems of community adjustment are somewhat different. He has no visible wound or injury to explain why he is back home while his buddies are still at war. Consequently, he wonders if people will think he is a slacker or a coward or a "gold-bricker." Unhappily, sometimes his fears are justified. An astonishing percentage of otherwise intelligent persons in the community possess an abysmal ignorance of psychiatric conditions and, because they fail to understand, are prone to ascribe them in others to lack of "guts," weakness of will, or some other equally erroneous factor. The psychiatrically discharged soldier and the psychiatrically rejected inductee both sense this prevalent community attitude toward the nature of their disability and suffer under its consequences. Moreover, some soldiers discharged from military service for psychiatric reasons are resentful and bitter over their separation from it since they, too, fail to understand the necessity for the discharge.

They do not see why they are no longer felt needed or wanted in the army; they perceive no connection between their occasional "black-outs" or fainting spells, their moods of apathy and depression, or their attacks of anxiety and panic and the nature of their military duties. They do not foresee—as their officers do—the strain-provoking experiences that lie in wait for them, the pressures that will be placed on their adaptive capacities by combat conditions; they do not see that their "black-outs," depression, or anxiety are warning, danger signals pointing to a fragility of adjustment equipment.

As a result of their failure to understand these matters many such men return home feeling guilty, as if they had deserted comrades in time of need; feeling that perhaps, after all, they are the slackers that many in the community assume them to be; and feeling most of all a compelling necessity to save their face. Because their psychiatric symptoms are not externally apparent, as an amputated hand or a crippled knee, some of this group deliberately manufacture physical reasons to explain their presence in the community. When asked why they were discharged they mumble something about flat feet or a heart condition or an impairment of vision or hearing. Occasionally some of them feel so ashamed of the nature of their difficulty that they conceal the reason for their discharge from their own families by offering some vague physical condition instead. Even if the family do come to know the real reasons for the discharge they, too, may feel the need for face-saving with neighbors or the other workers at Father's shop, and a sort of family conspiracy is agreed upon that the soldier is home because of a "strained back."

There is one point in his civilian adjustment, however, where the face-saving excuses of the psychiatrically discharged soldier cannot succeed. This is when a prospective employer asks to see his discharge papers. All subterfuges, no matter how innocently motivated, are now revealed, as the official document may state in blunt language that the man has been discharged because of "unsuitability for military service."

Theoretically, this official explanation might refer to any one of a number of different causes, but employment managers and personnel departments have come to assume that this phrase usually refers to some psychiatric condition.

Till the spring of 1944 the papers of a soldier discharged for psychiatric reasons were likely to have the reason stated as due to psychoneurosis, which made matters still worse in view of the widespread misunderstanding of this term and its implications, but that practice happily has now been abandoned. At other times the discharge papers may have been still more cryptic, with the cause for discharge merely checked against a code number. Sometimes this code number when deciphered by those "in the know" referred to discharge under Section II of the Medical Department, thus constituting a "certificate of disability," under which a majority of psychiatric cases left the service.

At other times the code number referred to Section VIII, which was a non-medical type of discharge. It was used to separate from the army a variety of men displaying what military officials call "inaptitude for military service." These may have included those who were psychopathic personalities, feeble-minded (mental defectives), or habitual bed-wetters or those with various behavior disorders. Then there was Section VI, which covered fraudulent enlistments, as well as Section X, which referred to discharge for a miscellaneous group of conditions lumped together under the heading "for the convenience of the government." Dishonorable discharges following courts-martial and civilian arrests were covered by still another section of army regulations. At any rate, employers quickly came via grapevine to learn the significance of the code and their pre-employing scrutiny became more rigid.

This industrial oversensitivity to anything smacking of psychiatric has become almost an obsession to some employers and is, of course, grossly unfair both to the ex-serviceman and to the industry that thus deprives itself of a valuable worker. Much of this book has been devoted, by implication at least, to debunking the prevalent superstitions and stigmata surrounding the whole subject of psychiatric disorders. By this time it is hoped that it has been made clear that the psychiatric reasons leading to discharge from military service (or leading to rejection at an induction center) are *disqualifications for military service only*. An overwhelmingly large percentage of men so labeled have performed efficiently in prior civilian life and can and will perform equally efficiently when they return to civilian life. The nature of their disability makes them poor military risks, to be sure, but need carry no implication of hazard for community participation. Blanket refusal of employment to this group solely because of a psychiatric discharge is both cruel and stupid. Each case should be studied on the basis of its own merits, and if necessary industry should obtain advice from competent psychiatrists as to employment suitability.

It is true, of course, that some psychiatrically discharged men have symptoms that may make their return to their old jobs hazardous. Men who have developed epileptic seizures constitute one example of this, and men with memory impairment, confusion, or forgetfulness resulting from the aftermaths of skull injuries may constitute another. Such instances are in the minority, and if these men cannot work safely at their old jobs, new and less hazardous ones can be found. The rank and file of psychiatrically discharged men will be found capable and worthy of any job that aptitude and other routine tests indicate within their range of skill, and the numbers of truly unemployable veterans will be few.

In the case of most men discharged for psychiatric reasons the acute episode that led to their separation from service has passed by the time they reach home. However, certain attitudes may persist to make community adjustment difficult. One of the more trivial of these may be an insistence that not only family and friends but the community as a whole regard them as heroes (which, of course, in a sense they are), and accord them suitable respect as persons to be set apart, revered, and granted special privileges. The more insecure a returned soldier feels at being separated from the group support he came to lean on, the more he will demand recognition as a former member of that group. He will wish credit given him for the dangers and deprivations he has been through and will be certain that no one who has not experienced the same things can possibly appreciate his sacrifices.

This attitude is understandable enough and quite human. It usually does not last very long, although some very insecure veterans may cling to it indefinitely. A grateful public will be tolerant of this attitude and will humor its owners unless or until their demands exceed reasonableness. This need to be thought of as a hero is one of several reasons why certain veterans postpone doffing their uniforms on returning home. It causes others to complain noisily and belligerently at paying customary civilian prices for articles they formerly purchased at canteens at a discount. It leads some to expect special privileges, such as being granted immunity to traffic regulations when driving a car, preference such as they had when they were in the army when it comes to queuing up for theater seats, freedom from the exasperations of rationing, or free medical, dental, or hospital care for postwar-contracted illnesses.

The need to be regarded as a hero displayed by an occasional ex-serviceman is at worst merely a passing annoyance to family or friends. When, however, such an occasional man bands together with thousands of other similarly minded ones and when their demands for special privileges are taken up by veterans' organizations and used as political sandbags, the situation may assume aspects of national importance.

Another familiar attitude expressed by some returned soldiers (but more likely by the dependent or immature, or by those with some disorder of personality) is that of chronic complaining. Literally nothing ever meets the full approval of such veterans. The more uncomfortable the pangs of civilian adjustment, the more bitter and varied become the occasions for their complaints. They gripe and they grouse about everything, and their families grow despairing at attempts to placate them. Most of all, they repeat monotonously their resentments at being sent into the service, at having to leave home when Tom, Dick, and Harry were deferred or rejected, at losing out on the fabulous war-industry wages, etc., etc., until they antagonize almost everyone who lends ear to their complaints. Such irritation may be largely overcome if family and friends understand that, with the exception mentioned below, most of this complaining should be interpreted as a symptom of an underlying difficulty in getting reestablished in community life. Corrective efforts should be directed to the basic difficulty of adjustment in general, rather than exclusively to the complaining.

The exception referred to concerns chronic complaining when it comes from that special kind of individual described in Chap. 5 as the psychopathic personality. Such persons seem to derive a perverse satisfaction in stirring up trouble. They are apt perpetually to carry a chip on their shoulders and to have developed overweening egos insatiable in their need for attention through any device whatsoever. The psychopathic personality was a psychopathic personality long years before he ever entered military service, and his prewar adjustment may have been continuously stormy and tumultuous. His army career was likely to have been characterized by the same turmoil, and now that he is back in the community his troublemaking propensities resume unabated. As was said earlier, little can be done to lessen complaints from such as these, and unless or until their behavior reaches antisocial proportions, when custodial care can be invoked, their families and the public at large have scant recourse except to bear with their malevolence as patiently as possible.

Last of all, we come to those problems of community adjustment of a group of psychiatrically discharged men whose disabilities are not severe enough to call for care in a mental hospital but nevertheless are sufficiently handicapping to postpone immediate reemployment or full entrance into community activities. These include men who suffer with a variety of emotional conditions less severe than committable insanity. Some are overly quiet, depressed, or apathetic, with little interest in anything. The family can stimulate in them no spark of animation, and not infrequently they may be discovered weeping. This kind of psychiatric casualty usually dislikes to leave the house and mix with others. It is hard to persuade him to attend parties or other gatherings, and often he will reproach himself for all sorts of fancied sins of omission and commission. A common self-accusation of this kind is his assertion that he has no right to happiness or comfort when he has been discharged and sent home while his buddies are still in combat overseas. His thinking, of course, is faulty, and the family should realize that it is symptomatic of the loss of insight his emotional disorder has produced.

Another frequently encountered reaction among this group of returned servicemen is constant anxiety. This can be expressed in dozens of different ways; some of the most common are restlessness, feelings of inner tension as if the man wanted to scream, indecision over a host of petty matters, and a state of generalized nervousness. Such men often have trouble in sleeping. They have insomnia, or their sleep is broken into short snatches and when they do get to sleep it is frequently interrupted by nightmares and terrors. At times during the day acute attacks of panic may arise for no discoverable cause, in which the men perspire profusely, complain of palpitation of the heart, breathlessness, and an awful certainty that they are going to die. Of course they never do die of such panic attacks and invariably the anxiety wears off, but few other physical or mental symptoms can compare with these for sheer terror and torment.

Then there are those other emotional conditions, described in Chap. 5, in which the returned soldier is morbidly preoccupied with a host of uncomfortable bodily complaints. Headaches, queer prickling or tingling or "drawing" sensations in head or neck, spots before the eyes, feelings of muscular weakness in arms or legs or perhaps all over, flutterings around the heart or stomach, vomiting, dyspepsia, tight feelings in the abdomen—one could run down the list of symptoms in a patent-medicine advertisement and find most of them duplicated in the complaints of this kind of psychiatric casualty. He insists that they are uncomfortable enough to prevent him from going back to work until they are relieved and he experiments with one remedy after another or goes to doctor after doctor. If such a man proves after a bit to be a sore trial to the patience and continuing sympathy of the family, let it be remembered that he is not faking or imagining these symptoms. As explained previously, they are very real; he is genuinely uncomfortable and he is truly convinced that there is some physical causation for them. Nevertheless, if, as in most such cases, no organic cause for them can be discovered, the explanation must be sought in the realm of his inner feelings, and the condition must be viewed as another of the curious ways in which certain persons express their difficulty in adjusting to some experience of life.

Closely allied to this kind of emotional disorder is another, in which a returned soldier with some actual physical injury persists in emphasizing its disabling features all out of proportion to the degree of disability to be expected. One such man with perhaps a moderate contracture of the muscles of a leg suffered from a burn may convince himself of the total uselessness of that leg and proclaim he cannot walk without help. Another may have lost part of the vision of one eye from a shell splinter but insists he is all but totally blind, etc. Again, let it be emphasized that these men are not goldbricking. Instead, they are thoroughly and genuinely miserable because of complicated things going on in the unconscious parts of their minds, which they do not understand and which make it necessary for them to exaggerate the seriousness of their injuries. And because the causes do lie in the unconscious part of their minds where they cannot get at them without skilled help, these men cannot "snap out of it" as their friends in exasperation urge.

Other types of psychiatric conditions that are not severe enough to require hospitalization but make community adjustment difficult until they are corrected include a variety of attitudes and mannerisms that perplex or annoy families and friends. For example, there is that obsessive tendency on the part of some to rehash monotonously over and over again certain topics or reminiscences until they completely bore their companions. There is also that condition which produces an attitude of extreme oversensitiveness to fancied slights or criticisms and results in sulking or a hurt withdrawal from further contacts. Suspiciousness and a conviction that others are out to take advantage of him are yet other attitudes that may retard a man's community adjustment.

One could go on for a long time describing an almost endless array of psychiatric conditions of these kinds. The point to be made, however, is this; the attitudes, the mannerisms, and the symptoms just described are all indicative of a disorder of personality and of adjustment equipment that has passed over into a moderately severe state. However, while few of these particular states are severe enough to justify admission to a psychiatric hospital, *they do need psychiatric treatment.* This treatment can usually be obtained on an outpatient basis, *i.e.,* in a psychiatrist's private office or at a mental hygiene clinic, and can be undertaken while the patient continues to live at home. Treatment is necessary, however—make no mistake about this—if the condition is to be corrected and prevented from degenerating into a chronic state. Families should not indulge in wishful thinking and hope that with the passage of time the condition will clear up itself. True enough, as time goes on some of the original symptoms do disappear, but they have a tendency to become transformed into other symptoms whose underlying meaning is identical with the first ones. Under proper psychiatric treatment many of these conditions can be helped, and such treatment should not be delayed.

Where can a discharged serviceman obtain psychiatric treatment? The first step is to ascertain whether the disability that resulted in discharge has been officially classified by military authorities as service-connected or nonservice-connected. If its origin has definitely been established as service-connected, then the nearest office of the Veterans Administration will arrange for treatment. If nonservice-connected, the local Red Cross is the best place to go to secure information as to how treatment can be obtained. In many communities there are psychiatric clinics supported by community chests or other private agencies where treatment can be secured. Likewise, many of the larger communities have one or more psychiatrists in private practice who will be available for treatment purposes. If none of these resources happens to be available in a given community, then a letter to the Director of the Division on Rehabilitation, National Committee for Mental Hygiene, 1790 Broadway, New York 19, N. Y., will bring information. This organization recently has prepared a Directory of Psychiatric Clinics and Related Facilities and copies may be obtained for twenty-five cents by writing to the address just given.

Lastly, let it be remembered that there is no disgrace in owning up to a psychiatric condition; that it is an illness just as some disorder of the physical body is an illness; that most persons with a psychiatric condition do not outgrow it if left unaided; and that proper treatment usually can do much to cure or at least lessen its effects. Above all, *do not delay treatment.*

Once a man is under treatment by a psychiatrist there are still many things that families and friends can do to cooperate with the doctor's treatment and thus hasten cure. First and foremost, do not jump to the conclusion that, just because the ex-soldier in whom you are interested has a disability labeled "psychiatric," he is suffering from some mysterious malady that sets him apart from other human beings. It may help to reread that portion of Chap. 5 which explains about this.

Adopt a natural attitude toward him. Merely because he is emotionally sick does not mean that he is helpless or should be excused from all ordinary responsibilities and courtesies. Bear with his eccentricities or irritabilities up to a reasonable point, but do not permit him to tyrannize over the family. Let him feel by your attitude that you understand and sympathize with him, but do not commiserate with him. If he starts in on a bout of self-pity try to change the subject or plan some diverting activity. Be ingenious; let him do as he pleases the first few days, but after that brief breathing spell commence planning with him along whatever lines may be indicated, finding a job, hunting up the old crowd, etc.

If one plan doesn't work, don't give up in despair but get busy with another. Don't pretend to agree (merely for the sake of humoring him) with plans or ideas of his that are obviously fantastic or impractical. Be realistic with him and try to insist that he be realistic, too. Don't become overactive in probing emotional sore spots with him. Let his psychiatrist take care of that delicate and dangerous process. If he shows no inclination to talk about his war experiences, don't try to force them out of him. He has reasons for his reticence or his inarticulateness on this subject that to him at least are good reasons, and he will only be driven to sullenness if he is probed against his desires.

Be on guard shortly after he arrives home to detect subjects of conversation that excite him or cause him to become hostile and aggressive. Once you discover what these subjects are try to avoid them. Don't be drawn into arguments with him. Listen to what he has to say, and then, even if you disagree within yourself and believe him to be in the wrong, change the subject or tactfully end the conversation. Hour by hour and day by day, let him feel that your attitude is a positive one, that you take for granted his return to health and normal life, and that, come what may, he can count on you forever and forever.

7

GOING BACK TO WORK

ONE of the most urgent problems of civilian adjustment facing the returned serviceman is the question of securing a job. Not only does the problem include the elemental aspects of his finding some gainful employment, but the individual man's attitude toward such employment likewise must be considered. Prior to the war, a few industrial organizations had begun a concentrated study of the attitudes of workers, but the necessity for wartime production swept aside most experiments of this nature. Now, however, with some eleven million men returning to their shops and offices with a newly discovered awareness of individual value and dignity, large-scale demands for attention to individual feelings and needs may properly be expected. It is all very well and very necessary for manufacturers' associations and chambers of commerce to address their thinking to the broader aspects of postwar industrial planning, but unless the human aspects of veteran reemployment are given equal consideration, broad planning will have little effect. Because in most cases the returned soldier is going to be different in many respects from the man he was before he went away, those differences are bound to stand out in as sharp relief in his job relationships and attitudes as they do in his home environment. They must, therefore, be understood and wisely dealt with by employers no less than by members of the man's own family. Likewise, the same reasons that make his adjustment difficult to his family and to his community make it necessary that he be handled with great tact and comprehension by his employer if he is to become efficient and productive, with minimal turnover, absenteeism, and intramural friction.

What are some typical examples of these very human and understandable attitudes that returned servicemen already have exhibited in industry? Job restlessness—a year or two of tramplike drifting from job to job before settling down—is one. Excessive demands for special favors and privileges based on the halo of military prestige is another. Still a third is a war-boom-engendered insistence on wage scales far out of proportion to an individual's actual industrial value. Also, there is the commonly encountered problem of near-neurotic choosiness in job selection, in which ambition overreaches vocational aptitudes. Attitudes of touchiness or even actual insubordination to industrial authority as personified by foreman or straw boss, who becomes identified perhaps with a formerly hated sergeant or corporal, make another problem of adjustment serious enough to merit managerial attention. Moreover, not a few ex-servicemen, in their efforts at postwar personal adjustment, are going to carry over into the shop and to their relationships there the grievances and disillusionments they are encountering in the outside community.

Naturally, these both can and do create friction and misunderstanding.

One could recount at considerable length additional problems connected with going back to work, but since this is a specialized field it will be well if discussion of it is left to specialists. Two eminent specialists of this kind are Dr. L. Holland Whitney and Dr. Matthew Brody of the Sperry Gyroscope Company of Great Neck, Long Island. This company is one of several pioneering industrial concerns taking an intelligent and serious interest in problems of human engineering. Dr. Whitney is the medical and service director, and Dr. Brody is the consulting neuropsychiatrist. Both have had extensive experience in dealing with problems of ex-soldier adjustment to industry, and both have received understanding and continuous support in their work from an enlightened management. Dr. Whitney and Dr. Brody, therefore, have prepared the following material on going back to work.

* * *

Into the caldron of war is thrown the finest of our manpower, and those who return from it are altered. A few are seemingly benefited by their experiences, but many more react unfavorably. The changes in some will be obvious and in others less perceptible. In some, the changes will be great and in others less. A grateful country will remember with honors in accordance to their deeds, and with pensions according to their needs, those who will have been rendered less capable of earning their livelihood by honorable service to their nation. They too will have the pride of having served. But gratitude, medals, pensions, and pride are not enough. The men who have made their sacrifices to preserve our way of life will want an opportunity to share in that way of life. However, they will find on their return that they will be employed not for what they have done but for what they are capable of doing. Those who cannot produce are entitled to sustenance by the government they served, and those who can are entitled to have their capability improved to the maximum possibility. The responsibility for this improvement must be shared equally by the nation, the community, industry, and the individual himself. If real efforts are made, the numbers of those incapable of aiding themselves will be materially reduced. That is the essence of rehabilitation.

In the post-war eras of previous wars few efforts were made to give the returning soldier an even break. In the period following World War I, our major efforts along this line were directed toward pensions. There were some sporadic attempts at vocational training and in industrial rehabilitation, but most of these efforts did not begin until a year after the war was over. The great majority of veterans were left to shift for themselves. The fact that most of them did well in this respect is no excuse for the repetition of such an unrealistic approach. We must be prepared to make our maximum efforts on behalf of the returned soldier as soon as he is returned. Such a policy, while perhaps initially expensive, will yield tremendous returns in material and human values.

The goal of rehabilitation is to bring a man to a point of maximal usefulness to himself and to society, to enable him to sustain himself and to enjoy the fruit of his production. The best criterion of success will be the ability of the soldier to obtain and to hold a job—not any job, but a good job.

Will I get a job? To the veteran who poses that question only a partial answer can be given. It depends on what he has to offer and on what the community and industry have to offer him. Whether or not jobs will be available in the postwar period will depend to a great degree upon the efficiency and rapidity of conversion from an essentially war economy to a peacetime one. One must frankly admit that present plans in this direction are vague and nebulous. We are only doctors and cannot pretend to understand the intricacies of industry, finance, and economics, but we do feel that any plan for reconversion that considers only the physical problems of buildings, machinery, and finance, without considering the fate of the present and future workers who are the people that must live during reconversion, is only half a plan and therefore inadequate. Retooling must be not only of machinery, but of man.

We doubt that all the present people employed in war industry will continue to be employed after the war. Many are superannuated, beyond retirement age, or ill and continue to work now because of the shortage of man power. Many will quit war work to return to former occupations now closed—as salesmen, clerks, accountants, and other fields in what is now considered nonessential work. Many women are now working because their men are in the services and will return to the home with the homecoming of the soldiers. This wholesale change in workers, plus the beginning of production of consumers' goods for which there is a large unsatisfied demand, should create many vacancies in industry. Whether these vacancies will provide work for all we do not know, but this much can be said, Federal law, union contracts, public opinion, and the desire of industrial management, all guarantee to the ex-soldier preference in employment.

When should the veteran return to work? A previous chapter has discussed the first weeks at home and the readjustment the returned serviceman must make in that time. The length of time required for this interval varies from person to person and depends to a great deal upon his physical, mental, and emotional state. The statement that the sooner the veteran looks for work the better is really placing the cart before the horse. The better the veteran is (as far as his readjustment is concerned) the sooner he will look for a job. With important exceptions, it has been our experience that the returned soldier who looks for a job within two or three weeks of discharge has the best chance of getting one and of doing well at it. This of course merely means that the man or woman who is adjusting well to himself and to life's problems cannot be content with idleness and will soon find himself employment.

We spoke of important exceptions. Occasionally we see a man who is obviously not well, either physically or mentally, apply for a job. Usually in these cases, some well-meaning but ill-advised relative or friend has urged him to go to work or the man has forced himself to go to work prematurely without understanding that one who is not well should not be working. He would do better to wait until his health is better before he attempts to work again. Going to work too soon invites failure and will lead to considerable and unnecessary discouragement, dissatisfaction with one's work and oneself, and a disgruntled attitude. We have seen other veterans who were far from well upon discharge but who had continued adequate care and medical attention until the maximum of recovery occurred. When they began working, they did quite well. Had they begun work earlier, they undoubtedly would have failed, and their failure would have been a disservice to themselves and to their employers. The community and well-meaning relatives should not be too prone to consider shiftless or lazy the veteran who is not working. They should understand that often the apparent unwillingness to work may represent an inability to work for unrecognized mental or emotional reasons. They should not hesitate to seek competent medical advice or even the services of a specialist in emotional or mental problems.

At work, the veteran will find things vastly different from what they were in the armed forces, yet what will disturb him most will be not the big things, but little things. In the armed forces, he was away from home, often lonely and worried about what was going on at home. He was without freedom and privacy. He was often exposed to danger or the threat of danger without any choice in the matter. He had to obey orders without question and accept at times indignities and repressions without comment. Griping, to a certain extent, permitted him to let off steam. The uniform and comradeship of his fellows gave him a feeling of being part of a successful fighting team.

Work habits in the armed forces are different. Most of his time, especially in training, was spent in preparation for events that seemed far off. Much of the preparation must therefore have seemed excessive. In time of battle, for example, when casualty rates may be high, many doctors, medical-corps men, and a vast equipment are immediately required. Before the battle, all these doctors and medical-department personnel and equipment must be ready, seemingly idle. Thus, for long periods of time spent in preparation, soldiers have little to do. Even extensive training after a while seems futile and unnecessary. The armed forces, because of their mission, work in spurts with long periods for preparation and recuperation. It is for this reason that military life has a reputation for making some people lazy.

In industry, men and equipment are employed more evenly. The difference between a maximum effort and between season lulls is insignificant as compared to what can occur in the armed forces. On the other hand, this even, uneventful, unthrilling routine will at first be an unbearable bore to those who are not used to it. At work, many of the restrictions of military life will have been removed, to be replaced by the unimaginative restriction of the time clock. At work there will be no commands; infraction of orders will not carry with it the threat of the guardhouse, company punishment, or the court-martial. There will be many other things that one will be expected to do or that one ought to do in order to get along with one's fellows. Most important, one does not have to take the guff from a foreman that one did from a tough sergeant. One can always quit or at least think of quitting a job. (In the armed forces, resigning is, to say the least, discouraged.) This does not mean that one *will* quit a job, but it is a comfort sometimes to know that one has that privilege. Sometimes veterans do that or take things out on their foremen, not realizing that what they are really trying to do is to get even with a sergeant, who brooked no arguments.

We can recall one veteran who became troublesome shortly after he secured employment. He would smoke when and where smoking was not permitted. When this was tolerated, he was noticed to loaf at his work. Finally he came late regularly and sometimes didn't come to work at all. When the foreman scolded him, the man brusquely and loudly quit his job. It so happens that there is a company rule that all men who quit must go through a certain procedure in the personnel office, similar in large measure to what applicants went through to get the job. The case under discussion illustrates the value of this procedure. The veteran turned out to be a sensitive, shy, easily hurt young individual, who had been discharged from military service for "nerves." His term of army service had not been a long one but had meant to him one continuous dread of being punished. He never was sent to the rock pile or the guardhouse, but he always was afraid that he might be. He came to fear authority, and in the army he had no chance to talk back. Finally his nerves gave and he "cracked up." His medical treatment was good, and he was much better at the time of his military discharge. What happened at work was this. Without realizing it, childishly perhaps, he so conducted himself that the foreman was forced to bawl him out. When the foreman, who was not expected to know all this, did so, this veteran was able to retaliate. He could quit and in that way show up the foreman. Essentially he was getting back at his old top sergeant, who he imagined had tormented him, by quitting on the foreman. When this veteran was helped to realize what was really behind his strange conduct, he at first felt chagrined. His attitude was additionally complicated by a long record of trouble in personal adjustment previous to his army experience. He was patiently helped in his readjustment and is now getting along very well with the same foreman, and he is no longer a special problem.

We should like to discuss in passing one type of veteran who cannot adjust to civilian work habits. He is fortunately in the minority. He is the restless, shiftless, irresponsible individual, who should not have been in the armed forces in the first place. Since early childhood, this person had never gotten along well with persons in authority. In school he was a truant, and in his youth, "wild." Often his history shows frequent clashes with the law, with numerous arrests. His story is one of restless wandering from one job to another, with no definite goal in mind, like flotsam on the sea of life. The more serious cases are the habitual criminals, who do not seem to learn from experience. They may be swindlers, card sharks, embezzlers, confidence men, or sexual perverts. Their glibness and engaging attitude make an initial good impression upon the inexperienced and gullible and enable them to worm themselves into positions of responsibility and trust. Their instability, however, makes it impossible for them to make good. The technical name for this aberration is "psychopathic personality," but it does not imply insanity. The severe, criminal, or sexual psychopath is usually rejected at the induction station. The milder ones will get by and in the services they constitute a continuous source of trouble. Occasionally they are capable of great acts of heroism, but they are not worth the trouble they cause. A classic example is the English officer who, at great personal risk, removed a time bomb and received a medal for his valor. Within a few months, he was court-martialed and imprisoned for a stupid, felonious swindle. Although these men are in the minority, they stand out like a sore thumb. In the services, when they are discovered, they are quickly discharged as troublemakers. Sometimes the real cause for discharge is given upon the discharge papers, but more often they are discharged for some other unrelated cause. These men, as a rule, cannot adjust in industry just as they cannot adjust to life's situations. Unfortunately, however, they are the loudest in their demands for special consideration as veterans. It is this type of veteran who spoils it for every other veteran who follows. A supervisor who has had one such psychopath working for him will be reluctant to try another veteran in the future. What must be remembered is that you cannot judge a herd by one black sheep. It is not fair to condemn the majority of worthwhile, conscientious, ex-servicemen because of the antics of a few. As a general rule, it is not worth bothering with these individuals. If they can be recognized, they should not be offered employment. If they get by the employment office, and they will with their smooth and glib attitude, they should be discharged when they begin causing trouble. Employers will find that the veterans' organizations will be the first to cooperate in weeding them out.

The handicapped man has a special problem in adjusting himself to a job. He must not only make the adjustments to civil work life demanded of all veterans, but has the added burden of a disability as well. Varying with the degree of their defect, persons can compensate (make up, adjust themselves) for their defects, depending upon their initial physical, mental, and emotional endowment as modified by their previous life experience. An individual with a dependent, self-pitying, helpless attitude toward himself and toward life will be floored by relatively minor handicaps. On the other hand, persons with a self-assured, self-confident attitude can compensate for much severer handicaps and even, in some instances, do better with their handicaps than they ever did before. Beethoven wrote music when he was deaf, and Milton wrote poetry when he was blind. It is not the handicap that determines what an individual can do thereafter, but the combination of the person and the handicap that counts. It is foolish to consider what the crippled can do; we must deal with human beings who are crippled. In the rehabilitation of the handicapped veteran, an equal role is played by (1) the veteran, (2) the community, and (3) industry, and there is no sharp line separating their responsibilities. No two can be successful without the third. The community (by that we mean the armed forces, Veterans Administration, various medical, social service, and educational agencies) is responsible for restoring the man to the point of maximum recuperation from his disability. This involves everything that happens to the man from the time of injury to the point of maximum recovery. Many injuries are only temporarily disabling, being such that, after treatment, the man can be restored to full duty. Other injuries make it impossible for him to continue in military service and will necessitate discharge. The treatment of this man should (and does) involve a great deal more than ordinary medical and surgical attention. It is not enough to merely provide him with an artificial limb, or a hearing aid, or insulin if he is diabetic. There is the responsibility to provide him, if possible, with sufficient skill to earn a living. In some this will not be possible, and they should be cared for by pension. If we were willing to devote sufficient effort and money at the beginning toward the restoration of the disabled man, the number of those who would have to rely only upon pensions would be greatly reduced. A program such as this might be tremendously expensive in the beginning but would in the long run be worth while, not only from the human point of view, but from the financial point as well. The cost of a totally disabled man includes not his pension alone but also what he does not produce and the job he does not hold. Community responsibility does not cease when the veteran is discharged from the hospital. It should then undertake to teach him a skill and to encourage him to take his part in the life of the community and in a job, if possible.

The most important role that industry can play is to give the handicapped veteran a chance. Industry also must not consider the man by his handicap alone, but must take into consideration the human being who has the handicap.

Perhaps the best manner of demonstrating how the entire situation can be handled is by way of illustration.

L. K., formerly a soda jerker, was inducted in the navy in November, 1940. Two years later his left arm was badly mangled in an automobile accident on shore, necessitating amputation just below the shoulder. After the initial shock had worn off, this young man became seriously depressed. His only means of livelihood involved the use of his arms, and he had lost his left arm in a most unprosaic manner, far from a field of battle. The Veterans Administration could not suit him with an artificial limb. They were either too heavy or too uncomfortable. Even an untrained observer could see that he was having a hard time getting used to the idea that his left arm was gone and could never be replaced. However, there were many positive signs in his favor. He had always been conscientious and a reliable steady worker, so that when the rehabilitation service of the Veterans Administration referred him to us, we thought he was a good risk. He was placed in training school under sympathetic instruction. To start him off, and mainly to demonstrate to him what could be done with one arm, we gave him a complicated packing job to do. This had formerly required the efforts of three girls working rather steadily, using both hands. The method-control department constructed a jig that held the part and turned it over when a foot pedal was used. With this jig (which has since been modified for use by normal girls), the injured man turned out by himself more work than the three girls had done. He not only was sure of himself, but he developed the idea that there was nothing that he could not do. Four months later, when he completed his industrial training course, he insisted upon being permitted to operate a turret lathe. It was obvious that he had gone to the other extreme mentally. His instructor permitted him to work on a turret lathe for a few days, until he was convinced that it required the full use of both hands to operate properly. Since he was so interested in this type of work, he was assigned to a milling machine, and a padded extension lever was attached to the left-hand control, which he could push with his shoulder. After a day or two at this, he seemed to be working under continuous strain. His foreman was quick to recognize this and sent him to the infirmary. The doctors there found that his stump was red, angry and bruised. This man had been too proud to admit that the way the work was arranged was too much for him. A new lever was arranged that could be pushed by the knee. Since then his work has been fully as satisfactory as that of any other man doing the same type of job. He no longer is in need of any special type of consideration. Incidentally, his personality has changed. He is self-assured and self-confident. The Veterans Administration now has an artificial limb for him that he will accept. It may be that this new limb fits better. It may also be that his mood has improved and he is now ready to accept his difficulty and has adjusted to it.

Let us recapitulate everything that went on as far as this man was concerned after the injury. Medical treatment saved his life but left him without an arm. Treatment by the Veterans Administration overlapped industrial employment. When he was first employed, it was obvious that he had not fully adjusted to his handicap, and a psychiatrist would say that he had a reactive depression, but full consideration showed that there were so many positive factors in his favor that a trial at employment was warranted. He required and received considerable encouragement and guidance during his training period. Then a job was found to suit him. The first placement was unsatisfactory, but this was soon recognized and further adjustments were made in his job to make it suit him. Throughout it all, he was treated as a person with a problem and not a number assigned to a machine. The veteran himself was sufficiently ambitious to be willing to cooperate. In this instance, there was complete cooperation between the veteran, the community, as represented by the Veterans Administration, and his employer. Each played his part and the result was satisfactory.

One cannot overemphasize the importance of the attitude of the veteran to his disability. An irritable, self-pitying "look what I did for my country—the world owes me a living" attitude, if permanent, makes rehabilitation impossible, because this person has been overwhelmed by his difficulty and cannot compensate for it. True enough, his defect may be such that there is no other way out for him. This type of attitude can best be overcome by early vocational therapy, pre-industrial training, a chance at a job, sympathetic understanding, and perhaps even some coddling when he first begins to work, gradually replaced by greater responsibility. The more promptly and efficiently such measures are instituted, the smaller will be the opportunity for the veteran to fall into a "cripple complex" type of mind. The greater the individual's difficulties in adjustment, the more thorough the efforts made on his behalf will have to be.

Another type of attitude sometimes seen is the blind refusal to acknowledge one's handicap. This is especially prone to happen where the handicap is less obvious or where there is childish shame over the disability. Such an unrealistic refusal to acknowledge reality is characteristic of the individual who like an ostrich buries his head in the sand and runs away from life's problems. This attitude may be illustrated by the following illustration.

Diabetes is a chronic disorder for which there is no cure but for which there are excellent remedies. A diabetic who takes care of himself and watches his diet and takes insulin if necessary can lead a perfectly normal life otherwise. On the other hand, a diabetic who neglects himself and will not stick to a diet is courting disaster. We were recently called upon to examine two young veterans who had been discharged because they had developed diabetes while in service. One of them was a bright, alert chap who always knew how to take care of himself and met this disability in a frank and open way. He learned how to test his urine, knew all about calories and diets, took his own insulin, and had himself checked regularly by the doctors in the Veterans Administration. This man was hired. He has done well in training school, and we are not in the least worried about his future. The other boy, however, felt ashamed of his ailment and deliberately tried to conceal it from us. He was always afraid that people might find out about it, as if that would make any difference. If he were at a party and they served ice cream, he would eat it rather than have people consider him different. His unrealistic attitude toward his defect was only another manifestation of an immature, irresponsible, and shiftless pattern of life. It is not our purpose to find fault with people, but if this boy had been hired and later cut himself, he would almost surely end up with a serious infection. Consequently he was not accepted.

The attitude of industry toward the employment of physically handicapped individuals is important. A positive rather than a negative approach is desirable. Management should decide these problems as they arise from the point of view of what the handicapped person *can* do rather than what he cannot do. If this is coupled with good job analysis and job placement and replacement, the numbers of those found employable would be tremendously increased. A handicap should practically never be considered a bar to employment. A handicap should rather be considered as a factor modifying the choice of a job. As a general rule, when a handicapped individual desires work, despite his defect, industry can assume that his personality and mental make-up are such that he will make a superior employee. Insurance carriers and companies that have had experience in employing the handicapped have found that such employees have as a rule better attendance, employment, and accident records than the general average. The problem of the physically handicapped veteran is little different from that of the man injured in civilian life.

The veteran discharged because of "nerves" is in a very similar situation. It is a defect that is not obvious, like an amputated extremity. These people have feelings of inadequacy and inferiority to begin with. This is not helped when discharge from the service gives them the notion that they have been cast aside as weaklings. People who are amateur psychologists "know" that fear plays a role, so that, to their simple notions, these veterans are really yellow or perhaps a little crazy. As a matter of fact, the proportion of medal winners is no lower among people suffering from nervous troubles than among the so-called "normal." Every individual has his breaking point. It is true that some are harder to break than others. Among those who seem to have broken down easily are individuals who would have made perfectly adequate adjustments in civil pursuits but whose temperaments were such that they could not stand up under the strain of military life.

The majority of the nervous veterans are individuals who were nervous before they entered military service. Their stories may not have been believed prior to induction, or at the time of examination they may have faked in reverse, masking their symptoms, or these symptoms may have been so covered up that they were not aware of their difficulty themselves. Be that as it may, unless they are given an opportunity to rehabilitate themselves, their feelings of insufficiency will become exaggerated to the point where they will be permanently invalided. The difficulty in working with these people is that their handicaps are of a nature that they usually cannot be seen or measured and are hard to understand.

In the emotionally handicapped person, the handicap itself may be the result of his inability to meet life's demands and situations and also satisfy his own internal needs. The emotionally handicapped individual usually does not know what he is running away from or what has warped his feelings or thinking, except that he does not feel or think right. He cannot evaluate himself as objectively as the physically handicapped person can. Where a veteran with a physical handicap cannot realistically accept his handicaps, the chances are that he is emotionally handicapped as well.

It has been our experience that a majority of these people are restored to a fair state of health and productivity merely by discharge from the army and return to old familiar surroundings. Others require considerable aftercare. As mentioned before, there is a tendency for a few to return to work too soon. This is a mistake. We do not think that they should return to work until their nervous symptoms are fairly well under control. On the other hand, industry will miss many a good worker if it is hesitant about employing men with this kind of defect or if it waits until they are completely cured.

Many nervous disorders occur in individuals who take themselves and duties too seriously or set too high a goal for themselves and are overly conscientious, worrisome, and extremely anxious to do a good job. This tendency is aggravated when we add the factors of fatigue, exhaustion, and lack of sleep to these traits. This is particularly true of people with stomach symptoms, certain types of depressions, and the "anxious" cases. While these personality traits are a handicap to the individual, the same traits are very valuable industrial assets. Psychiatrists will tell you that the advice they give this type of patient is to refrain from taking themselves or their jobs too seriously, because if they are unchecked, this type will try to kill himself with work. It is well known that many "nervous breakdowns" are alleged to be due to overwork. Actually overwork is the first symptom and not the cause. It reminds us of the story Dr. George S. Stevenson tells of a man who was applying for a job and thought he was doing very well until the boss asked, "Why aren't you in the army?" The applicant's heart sank as he was compelled to confess that he had duodenal ulcers. "Fine," said the boss, "I never knew a man that was worth anything that didn't have ulcers."

Employers may not realize it as well as this boss did, but they have been hiring people with nervous dispositions for years. There are no accurate statistics, but it has been estimated that at least eleven million persons in this country suffer from some type of nervous ailment even in peacetime. The amazing thing is not that large numbers of people are affected in this way but that most of these people are working, raising families, and discharging their duties as citizens in a more or less efficient manner albeit at a great cost in personal comfort.

The best criteria of a man's suitability for employment are (1) his school record; (2) his work record before he went into the armed forces; (3) his achievements in the armed forces; (4) how long it takes him to apply for a job; (5) his attitude to himself, his employer, and his disability, if any; (6) evidence of maturity and responsibility as shown by his marital status, savings, attitudes toward his dependents; (7)

his plans for the future; and (8) his reliability as indicated by his ability to stick to some job or endeavor. Employers should take into consideration the employee's age and background, because what might be a good work record in a boy of eighteen might be a miserable record in a man of thirty-five. They must also remember that in certain industries (as the building trade) and in certain rural communities, seasonal work is the rule. If all or most of these criteria are satisfactory in a veteran who is applying for a job, employers can usually disregard any history of a "nervous breakdown," irrespective of type.

The employer also can rely upon the judgment of the Veterans Administration or other government agency that might refer an individual as to his readiness for employment. Employment supervisors must at all cost beware of amateur psychiatrists, who may have half-baked and completely erroneous notions concerning nervous and emotional disturbances based upon half truths.

The veteran will want to know what his rights are under the law. Section 8 of the Selective Training and Service Act of 1940 is specific in what it states. Briefly stated, a returning veteran, whether inducted or enlisted, must be reemployed by his former employer in a position of like status, seniority, and pay, if: (1) he left the job directly for the armed services; (2) he applies for his job within forty days after discharge; (3) the position left was not temporary; (4) he is still qualified to perform his former duties; and (5) the firm's circumstances have not so changed as to make reemployment impossible or unreasonable. He may not be discharged for one year after reemployment without just cause. This section applies equally to the National Guard, Wacs,

Waves, Spars, women Marines, and by later legislation to the Merchant Marine. This law is enforced by the Reemployment Division of the Selective Service System. If a veteran has any difficulty in securing his rights, he may consult the reemployment committee of his local Selective Service Board for aid. In the event that he does not obtain satisfaction, this committee will be able to advise him fully on procedure for carrying his case further. It is unlikely that court action will be more than rarely required. Most employers will scrupulously obey the letter and spirit of the law.

Although the veteran is assured in most cases of his old job, he may not want it. As a rule, the seventeen- and eighteen-year-olds entering the service will not have had much of a job. After the passage of a few years, they will be reluctant to return to a job that looked so good after school. Certainly, Joe S., who was graduated from high school and worked for a few months as an office boy before entering the Air Forces, will not feel like going back to an office boy's job on his return with a commission. Then, too, many ex-soldiers and sailors will have learned a trade or skill in the service that will prove much more valuable to them than their old one. To those that desire it, there will probably be excellent opportunities for furthering their education at government expense after the war. These opportunities will undoubtedly include a chance at occupational and technical training. The veteran will have to figure out for himself whether he will want his old job back or a different one. He may want to get more training. He will be able to get advice from the Reemployment Division of the Selective Service System, from the United States Employment Service, and from the Veterans Administration. What he is going to do will depend a great deal upon his capabilities and his opportunities.

Some mention has already been made of the employers' responsibilities. Industry must expect to take an active part in the training of returned veterans. Training will have to be in two main directions: (1) technical training, to equip the returned soldier with the skill necessary to do the work required of him; and (2) retraining in peacetime work habits. It will be necessary to be patient at first and to coddle the veteran for a while as he is making his adjustments to peacetime pursuits. A tolerant, honest, and fair attitude will be most helpful. A continued paternalistic attitude is undesirable from the point of view both of management and of labor and will not be necessary.

Before industry can hope to train workers, it will have to have a clear idea of what types of jobs have to be done. This involves careful job analysis. Industry should study, at this time, all jobs from the point of view of their physical, mental, and even emotional requirements. Only after a job analysis is done can job placement be carried out. After a man is placed on a job, a follow-up should be done in a short time, for what may have seemed a proper assignment at first may soon prove unsuitable for unpredictable reasons. If so, there should be quick job replacement. Putting the wrong man in the wrong job will be harmful both to the job and to the man. When such a program is instituted, industry will find that handicaps will rarely prove a bar to employment. Usually some type of position can be found to suit each man, irrespective of handicap. Some handicaps will require sheltered jobs. For example, certain types of epileptics are employable, but it might be hazardous to utilize them where there is moving machinery.

Preplacement medical survey should place emphasis on evaluation of an individual from a physical, mental, and emotional point of view. This includes a careful medical history, past personal history, an inquiry into his work habits, and an inquiry into his emotional and mental state. Examination must include careful physical evaluation. It may also include intelligence testing, Rorschach and other methods of testing the personality, and a psychiatric inventory. These tests should be done not from a point of view of acceptance or rejection of employment, but rather from the point of view of estimating his potentialities and defects. With the information obtained by such a survey, it should be much easier to fit him into a properly selected job. To summarize, the problem of placement involves (1) a careful inventory of the individual as a whole, including assets and defects, physical and mental; (2) job analysis; (3) job placement; and (4) follow-up and job replacement if necessary.

Before the war is over and demobilization on a large scale begins, there is a great opportunity for progressive industry to study the problems in their own plants, preferably using a small group of veterans as a nucleus. A pattern may be established thereby that will prove of inestimable value when the confusion of general demobilization arrives.

The basis of personnel administration is the golden rule. If management would always treat their employees as they would wish to be treated, and vice versa, reemployment of returned veterans would entail few unsolvable problems. The time to recognize and handle all these problems is now, for a problem recognized is a danger half averted.

8

GETTING REACQUAINTED WITH
THE FAMILY

FOR purposes of simplification the word "family" as used in these pages is deliberately restricted to the wives and children of returned servicemen. More men serving in the ranks in World War II have been married for varying lengths of time prior to induction than in any previous war. It might be well, therefore, to begin our discussion of the problems of getting reacquainted with the family by talking first about men whose marriages antedated their military service by several years, leaving for a later portion those other problems arising out of hasty war marriages.

After the excited happiness of the first few days at home has given way to a steadier, more enduring variety, one of the first problems to confront the newly returned husband may be his wife's job. For various reasons, many wives took jobs on their husbands' departure. Some did it protestingly because there seemed no alternative way to make up the deficit in the family budget. They got jobs, not because they particularly wanted to work (indeed, many wanted just the opposite), but for the blunt fact that they had to. Other wives perhaps more affluent went to work not so much because of the wages it brought but because they grew bored to death when their husbands were away and they wanted something to keep them busy. Still others sought a job in war industry in response to a deep and genuine need to do their part in winning the war.

A surprisingly large number of wives, however, took jobs as soon as their husbands left for camp for the very human reason that they were not cut out for domesticity, had secretly chafed under it, and for years had longed privately for an acceptable excuse to set them free. Whether in office or shop they loved their job, they loved the new friendships it developed, but most of all they loved the feelings of creativeness and power and independence they never had been able to derive from housework.

Now, however, the husband has come home and the problem at once confronts them both: shall the wife keep on working or quit her job? In reaching a solution to this problem, mutual heartaches are likely and mutual compromises probably will have to be made. No general rule can be offered as a panacea, and each case must be considered on its individual merits. Of course, if the postwar period brings with it an industrial and economic slump the problem will be solved automatically for both husband and wife, since in that case thousands of women now employed in war industries will be discharged, and their return to a domestic status will become the only alternative.

Barring this possibility, however, the question poses itself: what attitude shall the returned husband take toward his wife's job? A partial answer will be found in the personality of the husband, no less than that of his wife. Just as various wives took wartime jobs for different reasons, so also will husbands view the retention of these jobs in various ways.

Some husbands, for example, oversensitive to real or fancied criticism from in-laws or neighbors, may issue peremptory orders that the job is to be abandoned pronto, even though they themselves may not as yet have returned to civilian employment.

Others, with perhaps a secret unsureness about their masculine prestige, may feel it a reflection on that shaky masculinity if their wives continue working, so they too command a return to domesticity.

Still others, basically dependent and possibly made more so by their military experience, may take quite the opposite attitude and become not only willing but eager for their wives to continue working.

A fourth group of husbands, mature, quietly confident of their essential masculinity and of their bread-winning abilities even in a postwar world, may take the sensible attitude of, "It's up to her. If she's happier on a job, then let her keep it."

If each side makes a sincere endeavor to see how the other one looks at the matter, most of these problems can be compromised. One possible exception may occur in cases where husband and wife each privately want different things out of marriage. Reference is especially made to the wife who found that she was just not naturally adapted to a domestic role and who also found herself married to a man whose conception of a wife was that of a *hausfrau*. There are many such men and women who have gotten themselves married to each other, and unless strenuous efforts are made to reach a compromise, marital happiness may be seriously endangered.

These people are not abnormal; at most they are merely mismated. Every woman has some masculine characteristics in her make-up just as every man has some feminine traits in his, and successful marriage depends in part on securing the proper combination. It is no disgrace for a woman to achieve the status of wifehood and motherhood but to have no aptitude for the traditional hearth-and-home environment in which these states are supposed to function.

In such instances, it is likely that she will prove a more contented—and, therefore, a "better"—wife and mother if she is permitted to find her satisfactions in a job outside the home rather than within it. Nor is it any reflection on his status as head of the family for a husband to modify some of his concepts of his wife as a *hausfrau* by agreeing to a continuation of her job. To do so may be difficult for some husbands, particularly those who built up while away an excessively domestically colored picture of "the little woman" bustling busily about the house with broom, dishrag, and dustcloth. But it can be done if mutual tolerance and compromise are exercised.

Another problem confronting the returned serviceman with a family is the renewal of his relationship with the children. Sometimes he can slip back into the old relationship with little trouble, but in other cases his absence may have done something to the feelings of the children that will require the utmost patience and tact to restore.

There is, for example, the boy who was nine or ten when his father departed for military service. Urged by the latter on leaving that now he must "take Daddy's place and become the man of the family," such a son may have followed these paternal admonitions with a vengeance.

Sergeant Anderson of a tank corps outfit returned home after two years in the South Pacific with a shattered shoulder and a medical discharge to find himself innocently supplanted by his young son. Deprived of her husband's affection and moral support, Mrs. Anderson understandably turned to Tommy for the satisfaction of these needs. With the best intentions in the world she misguidedly lavished on the boy not only the quota of love that ordinarily was his, but the additional amount that would have gone to her husband.

Naturally, Tommy, who was nine, reveled in this flood of affection. Because she was lonesome and sometimes afraid at night, Mrs. Anderson took him into the bed she had formerly shared with his father. Because she felt bowed down by responsibilities and often unsure of herself, she developed the habit of talking over her worries and doubts and uncertainties with the boy in an adult fashion just as if in reality he were the "man" his father urged him to be. And because he was so responsive and seemed to take responsibility so well, she failed to realize how much of it she loaded onto him and how much she came to depend on him. For practical purposes Tommy actually had become "the man of the family," and Tommy enjoyed it hugely.

When Sergeant Anderson returned home, however, he naturally assumed that he would take over and that Tommy would slip back gracefully into his former role of little boy. Consequently he was perturbed after the first few days at home to sense that his son behaved strangely toward him. He failed to understand, for instance, why Tommy cried so bitterly when he was sent back to his own bed in his own room; why he clung to his mother and almost glared when his father would kiss and caress her; or why he acted so sullen and resentful when his father tried to be friendly with him. It never dawned on Sergeant Anderson that his departing orders to Tommy to "take Daddy's place" had been obeyed literally and that his return home precipitated a jealousy situation that held within it all the elements of a family triangle drama.

Sergeant Anderson thought seriously about the problem confronting him. Upon remembering that Tommy had often written him about his stamp collection, he added to his son's collection whenever possible and discussed the hobby with him. He also encouraged the boy to talk about the activities of his class at school and about his friends. At intervals, the two of them went to basketball or football games, to activities that had a special masculine appeal.

It took Sergeant Anderson some months to restore the formerly healthy relationship with his son, but eventually he succeeded by dint of patience, understanding, and a vigorous effort to cultivate a palship with the boy. Sergeant Anderson's success, of course, was due to his intelligent interest in his son. The manner in which he rebuilt their relationship might not be applicable to a boy of a different nature. Each father who finds himself in such a situation must meet the needs asserted by the child's individual personality.

Daughters as well as sons likewise may figure in such jealousy situations.

Barbara Jenkins was twelve when her father was drafted. For several years previously her parents had been uneasy over the sullen, resentful attitude Barbara displayed toward her mother, and this was thrown into even bolder relief by the obvious favoritism she showed her father. Private Jenkins was relieved, therefore, when letters from his wife told of a change for the better in Barbara's attitude after his departure. Mrs. Jenkins wrote proudly of the girl's deepening affection for her, of a new considerateness she showed her mother, and of her helpfulness around the house.

But Private Jenkins had not been home a week when the old resentment flared anew. Barbara seemed to take a positive delight in quarreling with her mother and was fiendishly ingenious in experimenting with ways to make her unhappy. Both parents were dismayed, and Mrs. Jenkins was secretly horrified and tormented by guilt to sense after a bit a reciprocal resentment on her part toward her daughter.

What was happening was clear enough if one looked beneath the surface. As Barbara approached her teens an extra-powerful attachment to her father developed in which she unconsciously sought to capture him for herself. However, she was blocked in this by her mother, who naturally had first claim on him, and the girl gradually came to think (unconsciously again) of her mother as her rival. On her part, Mrs. Jenkins likewise sensed, in the unconscious realm of her mind, the competition of her daughter.

The departure of Private Jenkins for military service healed the breach for the period of his absence. So long as he was away neither woman could have him, and consequently there was no point in continuing the feud.

When Private Jenkins returned, however, the old rivalry was renewed, and Barbara's behavior toward her mother became understandable. All this was explained to Mr. and Mrs. Jenkins by the psychiatrist to whom they had gone for help with the problem, and by a judicious blending of tact, patience, and restraint of feelings on their parts, the girl was helped in time to work through her problem.

Much the same situation arises when the returned serviceman happens to be an older brother. Many a younger brother was elevated by the rest of the family to the role of senior when his older brother went into the army. Perhaps the kid brother was moved into the older one's room, allowed to wear some of the latter's civilian clothes, and given numerous privileges that ordinarily would not have been granted so long as the older brother remained at home. He would have been something less than human if he failed to enjoy this promotion, and likewise, he would be something less than human if he failed also to resent the demotion necessitated by the older one's return. Perhaps, too, the returned brother secretly resents the usurpation of his former role as the elder and finds it hard on returning to conceal *his* resentment. Much tolerance and understanding on the parts of the whole family will be required to prevent friction and unhappiness under these circumstances.

After some time away from home, the returned service-man may find that he and his wife no longer see eye to eye as completely as before about a number of family matters. Questions of finances may be a case in point. Living in a military environment, where almost everything was provided for him and where encouragement was given—by implication, at least—to an attitude of depending on Uncle Sam for ordinary needs, a returned soldier may find it difficult at first to agree with the careful budgeting his wife was compelled to devise. His sense of monetary values may have undergone a change, so that he construes his wife's repeated cautions about expenditures as parsimoniousness and nagging.

Another case in point where he and his wife no longer are in accord may concern her relationship with her parents. Some wives, a bit immature perhaps, never wholly emancipated themselves from emotional dependency on their mothers even though they may have been married some years. With the husband's entrance into the army many a wife of this type went back to live with her people and resumed an existence that for all practical purposes was identical to that of her premarriage days. When her husband returns she may feel inwardly inadequate to assume independent living with him away from the emotional support and dependency she developed on her mother. In such instances, the wife may unconsciously fear to leave her parents' rooftree and find all sorts of ingenious—but plausible—excuses for persuading her husband to live with her at her mother's and father's.

Of course, the same situation may arise in reverse with a returned husband who himself is somewhat immature and dependent on *his* mother, with the result that he is the one to seek plausible reasons for resuming civilian life in the home of his parents. Unless one of the two marriage partners is quite immature and quite unable to function adequately without parental support, or unless there is a genuinely realistic reason—not a cleverly rationalized one—for so doing, it is usually better for the newly reunited couple to resume married life alone.

Perhaps the greatest difficulty in relationships that confront the returned serviceman and his wife is the subtlest of all. This arises when one of the two grows more rapidly in his emotional development during the husband's absence than the other. Usually, though not always, it is the husband who does this as a result of the broadening experiences of his military life. As a rule, men and women select each other as mates, consciously or unconsciously because they sense the other possesses certain personality characteristics they need to off-set or to round-out their own. Thus, an emotionally immature and dependent man may, without consciously realizing why he does so, select a strong, aggressive woman out of his intuitive knowledge that she will mother him. And thus, also, a woman of this kind may with equal unawareness of the underlying reasons, select a passive, dependent man because of her need to mother him. So long as this balance of needs remains stable as it did on the day of the marriage, all goes smoothly and the couple are well adjusted to each other: *i.e.*, the needs of each are met in the other, and their respective rates of emotional growth or maturity proceed harmoniously at the level of the marriage at its outset.

But if or when one of them begins to have his or her rate of growth speeded up by any one of a variety of circumstances this former balance is upset. The soldier comes in contact with many persons of different minds and interests; his geographic horizon is widened and often his social horizon as well; dormant qualities of independence or leadership may be developed; he may come to gain a new, more adult concept of himself. If these things should happen to a man who went into the service as a passive, dependent personality needing mothering from his wife, he may grow irritated when the latter attempts to resume her mothering. In other words, the emotional maturity of this particular soldier has grown during his absence from home and unless his wife likewise has developed in this respect it may be troublesome for them to regain the old relationship.

The pangs of disillusionment at discovering that home life is different from what he expected assail the returned husband as keenly as they do the unmarried man. Wives awaiting their husband's return come in likewise for their share of disillusionment. Letters, curiously enough, are one reason for this. No matter how verbal and articulate, letters can never give a completely true picture of feelings, and unless the recipient is stolid and unimaginative he is bound to read between the lines and endeavor to find there what he wants to find. Wishful thinking, therefore, plays an important role in the interpretation of letters, but, like most wishful thinking, it seldom checks with all the realities when these eventually materialize.

A special disillusionment is likely to be in store for the wife of a returned soldier if she happens to be the kind who previously had placed an extra high value on the romantic aspects of marriage and on frequent demonstrations of husbandly tenderness. War is a grimly realistic business. The soldier is taught deliberately to kill and to harden himself against softer thoughts. A military environment offers few encouragements to the finer amenities of living, and not only does speech become crude but a man's very philosophy loses much of its former romanticism in favor of stark reality and an ability to cut through directly to the heart of a matter, brushing aside ruthlessly all nonpertinent facts.

Thus, in spite of a genuine affection for his wife a returned soldier may find himself—in contrast to his former outgoingness in this respect—strangely undemonstrative and brusque. He finds himself unable to indulge in the old tendernesses of speech or manner, unable as of yore to participate in rose-colored visions or to reciprocate in his wife's impractical but happy daydreams for the future. His war-engendered facility for seeing only the realities of a situation and for going straight to the point may cause him to appear unsympathetic, and, unless she understands the reasons for it, his wife may feel hurt and bewildered over the change in him.

Moreover, he may bring back an attitude that she as well as others in the family construe—erroneously—as a streak of hardness and immunity to human suffering. Reference is made to that philosophy of fatalism that combat experience develops in military men in which they take not only the attitude of "what is to come, will come," but use *"c'est la guerre"* as an expression of resigned helplessness to alter the inevitable. Thus, the wife of First Lieutenant Hamilton, former copilot of a B-17 bomber, who had seen many men die, may be distressed at his seeming cold-bloodedness in receiving her news that old Mrs. Henderson down the street is dying of cancer. "Too bad," he remarks briefly, "but there isn't anything we can do about it. What are we having for dinner tonight?"

SOLDIER TO CIVILIAN

Such attitudes as Lieutenant Hamilton's reflect neither callousness nor indifference to human values, nor do they indicate that those who express them have grown hard or cruel. Instead, they arise out of battle-born realizations that when one is truly helpless to influence a situation there is little to be gained by pouring out one's feelings onto it. Acceptance of the inevitable, refusal to mourn unprofitably for what cannot be helped or for what already has come to pass, and an insistence on trying to adjust to the present rather than to dwell on the past, is the stern and Spartan philosophy with which many soldiers return. It is a philosophy usually foreign to their prewar selves and is strange and disquieting to their wives. But it is the philosophy without whose support many would have been unable to carry on as good soldiers in the face of ghastly combat experiences and, therefore, is the philosophy that many will bring back to civilian life. Wives will be comforted to realize that in time it will give way in most instances to one better suited for civilian living and that their husbands are not the strangers to soft and tender emotions they appear to be.

Another disillusionment to some wives emerges from the displays of gruffness, disinterest, and boredom shown by certain returned husbands. There are various explanations for this, but seldom should it be interpreted as a genuine loss of love. One explanation is simple, and if the wife shows tolerance and unruffled patience the situation will correct itself. This explanation goes back to an understanding of the kind of military environment that was apt to be exclusively a masculine way of doing things. After a time this environment got into the soldier's very blood and became an integral part of him. But now he has left it and is back home. He loves his wife and he takes pleasure in her company, but his military life has left its imprint on him. Her ways of doing things are not the army's ways; her friends made in his absence are not yet his friends; her feminine logic in viewing a problem or of reaching a conclusion is not the masculine logic with which he is familiar; her abhorrence of his crudities and the latrine humor that had become second nature to him at first amuse, then annoy him; all in all he has his moments when he feels fed up with home and his wife, and bursts of gruffness and inconsiderateness are the outward evidence of this.

Fortunately, in most cases this will pass as he becomes more deeply enmeshed in the processes of redomestication, but until this process does become complete his attitude may cause his wife some unhappy moments.

If she is wise she will not insist that he devote all his time to her. She will learn to recognize the warning symptoms that announce he has not yet fully accepted his new civilian status and that there are times when he longs to get away from domestic cares as well as joys. At such times she will urge him to look up some of the "boys" and to take an evening or so in a wholly masculine environment. His eagerness to accede to her request will not mean loss of affection for her, but merely a temporary homesickness for a rough-and-ready type of existence that once held meaning and value for him.

What now about the returned soldier who comes back to a war bride whom he scarcely knows? His problems in some respects not only are different from those of men who had become accustomed to marriage before they went into service, but also are apt to be more difficult. In the first place the serviceman who married on the eve of being shipped overseas is likely to be chronologically younger than his buddy who had been married for several years. He is not likely to have had the measure of life sophistication of the older man; he is apt to be emotionally less mature because perhaps he has had insufficient time in which to complete his process of emancipating himself in his feelings from childhood dependency on his parents. If he is still—emotionally speaking—in the stage of adolescent development it is possible that he is impulsive and unreflective, and his hasty war marriage may be one indication of this. Should his war bride be equally immature, then the marriage in at least its more sober and responsible moments, is apt to be a marriage of children, bewildered, indecisive, and inwardly frightened at what they have done.

Observations on differing national cultures indicate a significant comparison between the degrees of emotional maturity of American boys of eighteen (the age at which they become liable for military service) and European boys of the same age. At eighteen years of age many American boys are still in the process of weaning themselves away from their childhood fear and dependency on their fathers. The American way of life has been such as to prolong their period of childhood shelter and protection against the impact of adult realities with the result that when they reach military age they are less free than the European boy, for example, from conflicts of mingled feelings of resentment and dependency on their fathers.

When such an American adolescent goes into the army or navy he may delude himself that he is at last severing the final bond of parental control and that now he is free and independent of family influence. Actually, of course, the reverse proves to be true. He soon finds that neither emotionally nor realistically is he any freer from dominance and dependency on parental figures than he was at home. All he has succeeded in doing is to exchange the dominance of a real father for the dominance of a symbolic one in the form of sergeant or commanding officer or in the form of military rules and discipline.

When finally he leaves the army this dominance that has perpetuated his dependency suddenly is removed, and for the first time in his life the returned soldier finds himself technically free. This word "technically" is used advisedly, for while chronologically this kind of ex-soldier is a man, emotionally he remains the adolescent he was on entering service, with the remnants of childhood dependency still clinging to him and with all his secret fears of assuming adult responsibility assailing him.

If he happened impulsively to have married just before entering service or perhaps while on furlough, he now returns to find himself faced with adult responsibilities that may overwhelm him. It is quite possible that his marriage in the first place was in part an unconscious attempt to convince himself (and others) that he was grown up and independent of parental control, a sort of disguised gesture of defiance against those parental forces which he thought were keeping him in bondage, his way of demonstrating to the world that he really was an adult. It is quite possible also that his girl married him for similar reasons on her part.

At the time it all seemed a grand and glorious adventure. Flushed with his newly endowed role of departing hero he swept aside as inconsequential all practical problems of marriage. The future, if it was envisaged at all, held no terrors for him, since he was blissfully ignorant that terrors might lie in wait. The need for patience in marriage, for tolerance, and for bearing with the frustrations of passing whims were needs that his adolescent immaturity had never been required to adjust to and consequently played no part in his marital anticipations.

But now he is home; *i.e.*, he is back in his home town but not in any house or apartment that he and his war bride had ever had time to call "home." Chances are that immediately after their hasty honeymoon the soldier went back to his outfit, leaving his new wife to continue living with her parents or with his. One of his first problems on returning, therefore, involves a decision of the practicalities of independent living. Finances play an important role in determining this, but other factors likewise affect the decision.

The extent to which the returned soldier may be genuinely independent in his feelings, and his degree of freedom from dependency on parental relationships may well prove additional factors. Even though the man actually is still dependent on these relationships, he may be under a need to disprove it by setting up an independent household establishment and leaving the parental roof. Sometimes this works out well in the end and sometimes not. In either event he finds the process of assuming adult responsibility an irksome one, particularly if the young couple have a new baby.

The dismal end results of one such situation are typified by Pvt. Patsy Larocco and his wife. Patsy was the youngest of nine children and his mother's favorite. As a youngster he was somewhat spoiled and accustomed to being absolved from household chores. In early adolescence he developed what his disgusted father called "big-shot ideas" as manifested by his attempts to act grown up beyond his years. Patsy was willful and heedless and insisted on leaving school in the seventh grade in order to get a job and earn his own money. He selected for companions only older, more sophisticated boys, and he was forever talking "big." At seventeen he announced he wished to enlist in the navy, and reluctantly his parents gave consent.

At a USO dance one night Patsy met a vivacious girl and began a whirlwind courtship terminating three days later in marriage. After a week's liberty Patsy was shipped out again and months later in Saipan sustained wounds that led to his discharge. Patsy also had left his new wife pregnant and, since she had been brought up in a children's institution on being abandoned by her parents, she went to live with the senior Laroccos. They didn't like her and they didn't like the new baby, and when Patsy returned his father lent him money to rent a flat down the street and to buy furniture.

At first all went well. The young couple with their baby were like children playing house together. But the responsibilities of domestic life not only were new to Patsy but began to chafe him. He was now almost twenty years old, but for all practical purposes he was still an adolescent, despite his swaggering and his verbal boasting. He didn't like to be awakened at night by the baby's crying; he liked less having to change its diapers; he resented his wife's requests for help with the dishes when he wanted to shoot pool; he grumbled when they had to stay home from the movies because no one could be found to stay with the baby; he couldn't see why his wife protested when he surreptitiously abstracted household money from the sugar bowl to place a bet on a "sure thing" at the race track; and he went into a furious rage once because she was so inconsiderate as to come down with the grippe just the day before they were to have taken a long-anticipated week end at the lake.

All the multitudinous irritations and pinpricks of marriage crashed down on Patsy like a ton of bricks. It wasn't at all what he had pictured it to be. He never had contemplated these hundred and one practicalities when he thought about getting married, and the need for assuming an adult role was too much for his immature state of emotional development. And so, like four-year-olds squabbling in a sandbox, Patsy and his wife grew increasingly miserable until at last he could stand it no longer and one night solved the problem (to his satisfaction at least) by packing a suitcase and disappearing from home.

Other reasons for the failure of some hasty war marriages to work out are to be found in the differences of emotional maturity of the two partners as discussed a few pages earlier in reference to men whose marriage had antedated their military service by several years. The broadening experiences of military travel and of meeting overseas girls of different educational or cultural backgrounds from those of his wife may have opened the eyes of the new war groom to the possibilities of a different kind of feminine companionship of whose existence he previously was ignorant. As a result he may find himself on his return making secret comparisons that not only trouble his conscience but which he may not be able wholly to conceal. This seems especially likely to happen to certain young officers whose military rank gave them access to homes and to social groups whose cultural coloring was different from that of themselves or their wives.

Second Lieutenant Frederick Wilson is an example. He came from a medium-sized town in Ohio, where his father worked in a factory. Fred's home was a modest one; by dint of some sacrifices the family had been able to put him through high school, and on graduation his highest ambition was to become a foreman in the plant where his father was employed. He wasn't particularly bookish, nor had he ever shown interest in music except jazz. He took no interest in politics or in international problems; he pared his nails with a pocket knife, came to the supper table in his shirt sleeves, and lived from day to day on a comfortable and superficial level of taking his pleasures as they came. Fred wasn't boorish or uncouth. It was just that his life experiences had been limited, he acted like everyone in his acquaintance did, and so far as he was concerned he neither knew nor cared that any other style of living was likely.

When the war came along Fred, then barely twenty, got the idea of applying for officers' training in the Air Force. He was accepted, and because he was naturally intelligent and deft he won his wings and was commissioned as a fighter pilot. A week before leaving for camp, however, Fred married the girl he had been going around with for the past year. Martha was a nice girl who had left high school in her third year to earn money for the care of an invalid mother. She, too, came from a modest family and was wholly content with the humdrum interests and recreations that appealed to Fred. Everyone said it was an ideal marriage; they were deeply in love with each other; they both had the same innocent but perhaps limited interests, and both had grown up together in the same narrow but comfortable small-town atmosphere. To Martha and Fred the Atlantic Charter was all Greek. A Mozart sonata bored them, although they did like the rhythm of Gershwin's "Rhapsody in Blue."

Martha and Fred were not stupid; it was merely that they were satisfied with their mode of life largely because neither had known any other. Fred wasn't particularly interested in the causes for the war—it all seemed so remote—but he was crazy about flying and he made a good pilot. As an enlisted man he was popular and enjoyed the rough-and-ready existence of camp life. He participated in the crude practical jokes of his buddies, cursed and swore automatically with them, and was none too careful about his grammar, although he had taken a prize in high school in English.

However, his elevation to the status of a commissioned officer changed Fred a bit. The changes were few and slow to come about at first, but when he went overseas they developed rapidly. He found himself thrown in with many men of college background and on several leaves for rest periods he was the guest of English families of culture and distinction. In this new world people talked about books and music and international matters with familiarity and lack of affectation, and Lieutenant Wilson listened respectfully and eagerly. New vistas began to open up to him and dormant sensitivities became sharpened. After a time he even ventured—timidly at first—to participate in conversations about subjects that a year previously were foreign to him and to his surprise found that he enjoyed it.

But one day a bit of flak caught him in the shoulder and ended his flying days. Lieutenant Wilson was shipped back to the States, given a medical discharge, and returned to Ohio, to Martha, and to the old job at the bench in the factory.

But it wasn't the old Fred Wilson who returned. For a few weeks he seemed to be, truly enough, his former self, but the adjustment began to grow difficult. For one thing, in spite of wartime wage schedules his old job paid considerably less than he had received from his former flying pay. For another, he felt a sort of job letdown after the glamour of flying. Also, he became aware of a feeling that he reproached himself for harboring: snobbishness toward the other men in the shop.

Most of all, however, he was troubled about the comparisons he found himself making between his wife and some of the women he had met overseas. It all added up to a mounting feeling of discontent that caused him to act irritable and moody.

Fortunately, Martha was a sensible girl with more than the average quota of feminine intuition. Sensing something of what was going on in her husband's mind, she waited until a propitious opportunity arose and talked it all out with him. It proved a relief to Fred to be able to pour out his jumbled, unhappy thoughts about the matter, and he was grateful to his wife for her understanding attitude that held no measure of condemnation in it. Because of her genuine interest in her husband's point of view, they continued to discuss possibilities of a new and richer way of living. Happily, Martha also had a good share of intellectual curiosity. She had had no provocation to exercise it before this time, but now she was anxious to go forward with her husband. They gradually worked out practical plans for self-improvement. Fred started to study a phase of his work in which he felt he had talent. Martha began to develop her individual taste in reading and started the study of music.

Finally Fred reached the point where he qualified for a more promising job in a distant city. So they set out with the anticipation of forming newer, more interesting friendships and discovering new activities. At last reports ex-Lieutenant Wilson and his wife are happy in their new location, and the adjustment seems to have been achieved.

And so we come to an end of this endeavor to discuss some of the problems of adjustment confronting returned servicemen and their families. If the aftermath of World War I can be used as a criterion, we can expect that eventually a majority of the eleven million or more men in military service will make this adjustment with reasonable satisfaction to themselves and to the communities in which they live, but in the process many heartaches will arise and some men will remain emotional cripples for the rest of their days. A genuine understanding on the part of families and friends will hasten this adjustment and in some instances may avert chronic social invalidism. To help bring about such a measure of understanding has been the chief purpose of this book.

The help to be found in any book, however, must of necessity be generalized. Many problems are certain to arise that cannot be covered within the scope of a single volume.

Where, then, can wives, parents, or the returned soldier himself turn to receive help with some specific difficulty of adjustment?

If the problem involves a definite psychiatric disability such as was discussed in Chap. 5, the Veterans Administration or the Red Cross or a local psychiatric or mental hygiene clinic is the place to seek help.

However, literally hundreds of thousands of adaptive problems will be encountered that affect the family relationships of the ex-serviceman but that do not come within the official classification of "psychiatric." In such cases one excellent place to receive counseling advice or assistance is the local Family Welfare Society. In more than two hundred communities both large and medium sized throughout the country will be found such social agencies. Sometimes they are called Family Welfare Societies and sometimes The Family Service Society or a similar name. Most are affiliated with a national organization known as The Family Welfare Association of America (122 East 22d Street, New York 10, N. Y.), and they are staffed usually by professionally trained social workers who have had training and experience in personal counseling. Although some have the word "welfare" connected with the title, this need cause no one to fear being stigmatized as a "charity" case. Most of these social agencies are privately financed by community chests or from other private sources and seldom have any connection with public agencies like municipal departments of public welfare.

Other social agencies besides those designated as Family Service Societies also will be found in many communities equally able and eager to be of adjustment service to the returned serviceman and his family. At any of them personal problems can be discussed in professional confidence, and, if the agency itself is unable to meet some specialized need, its staff workers will know where such a special help can be obtained. No hesitancy should be felt in availing oneself of the service that these organizations are prepared to give.

As stated at the outset of this book, it is human to have to face problems of adjustment; no one is immune from this necessity, and, when a problem is encountered that is too complicated to solve unaided, it is merely common sense to consult an expert. This is what one does with problems of sickness when one consults a doctor or with a legal problem when one seeks the help of a lawyer. This also is what one should do with a problem of personal adjustment when efforts at self-help have come to naught.

No book can outline specific steps on how a person might treat any or all veterans. After all, each man is a distinct individual, and his reactions to his experiences are to a great extent dependent upon the manner in which he reacted to varying experiences previous to his induction. His treatment needs should be determined by the facts of an adequately compiled case history that brings out many experiences of his earlier life. And a psychiatrist or a professionally trained social worker is usually the most competent person to undertake this.

Families of ex-servicemen should carefully investigate the backgrounds of people who claim to be authorities on the subject of rehabilitation. Generalities and snap judgments on the problem are likely to be dangerous. The most important aim of people who sincerely wish to aid in the readjustment of returned soldiers should be to achieve the greatest possible understanding of the complex experiences in which the soldier was involved during his term of service. This in itself will go far toward producing the intelligent and sympathetic atmosphere so essential to the veteran's first few months in civilian life.

The use of common sense and patience cannot be stressed too much. Those who view veterans with exaggerated sentimentality are apt to be among the first to lose interest. It must be kept in mind that the aftermath of the war is of equal importance with the period of actual warfare and that the well-being of veterans with disabilities is of no less importance than the physical and mental condition of soldiers entering combat.

It is hoped that there will be many in this country who will contribute valuable time and effort to community projects for aid to returned servicemen. To give such persons a primary outline of possible community organization, the National Committee on Service to Veterans has provided "Community Services for Veterans: A Guide for Planning and Coordination." It is reprinted in full in the following pages.

From such cooperative planning will come America's solution to one of the most gigantic problems we have ever faced.

COMMUNITY SERVICES FOR VETERANS

A Guide for Planning and Coordination

Prepared by

NATIONAL COMMITTEE ON SERVICE TO VETERANS

UNDER THE AUSPICES OF THE
NATIONAL SOCIAL WORK COUNCIL

FOREWORD

THE prospect of having more than fourteen percent of our population serving in the armed forces during the war has focused attention on the problems that will arise in connection with demobilization. As a result more than one hundred organizations, public and private, have indicated their intention to render services to veterans.

The Retraining and Reemployment Administration has been created by the President for the purpose of planning and coordinating the activities of governmental agencies dealing with the ex-service group. On the part of non-governmental organizations, there is a need for planning and coordination to avoid competition among the organizations and confusion and bewilderment for those to be served.

As an aid in this situation, officials of a number of nongovernmental national agencies which have as their concern the administration and planning, locally and nationally, of public and private health, welfare, and recreational services have formed the National Committee on Service to Veterans under the general auspices of the National Social Work Council. The functions of this committee are assisting in over-all planning to assure adequate service to veterans; providing advice and information to national private agencies about service to veterans; offering guidance to communities through local agencies and councils of social agencies; and consulting in an advisory capacity with governmental agencies.

SOLDIER TO CIVILIAN

This committee has made a study of the problems to be anticipated and has reviewed the history of experiences following World War I. Consideration has been given to plans already operating in many communities and to the program of the Retraining and Reemployment Administration. As a result of its studies and conferences with the leaders of interested governmental and private organizations, the committee has prepared this bulletin as a guide to planning community services to veterans. Millions of war workers will be discharged from industry during demobilization. Community plans for the assistance of veterans, suggested in this bulletin, will also be useful for assisting war workers.

SECTION I. THE RETURNING VETERAN

IN PLANNING national and local services to veterans of the armed forces, the number of veterans, the rate of discharge, and the individual needs of these men and women are among the factors to be considered.

The effective strength of the Army, Navy, Marine Corps, and Coast Guard is now fixed at 11,300,000. Approximately 1,500,000 men and women have been discharged from the armed forces since Pearl Harbor. It may be presumed that discharges from the armed forces will reach or exceed 1,000,-000 a year. If for purposes of estimating, it be assumed that the war will continue another two years, approximately 15,-000,000 men would have been in service by the close of hostilities.

In view of the number of discharges now occurring, it may be said that demobilization is under way now. The discharge rate will increase as hostilities end in any one or more theaters. Should the war in Europe end before the war in the Pacific, the size of the armed forces will probably be reduced for completion of the conflict with Japan. Further demobilization would then take place. With the end of hostilities in all theaters, full demobilization would follow.

The rate of discharge during the period of full demobilization has not been fixed. It will be affected by "the adequacy of transportation facilities, the time required by the mustering out process, the social and political pressures for a very rapid demobilization." [1] The rate may vary from 300,000 to

---

[1] Brookings Institution pamphlet, "Post War Reemployment," pp. 5-6.

500,000 a month. The armed forces required after hostilities cease may be a minimum of 1,500,000. Full demobilization after cessation of all hostilities, therefore, may take from one and a half to two years. Should the war continue another two years, demobilization would not be completed before 1948. Many variable and unpredictable factors will affect the rate of discharge. The possibilities suggested in this statement must be regarded, therefore, as unofficial and tentative. They are suggested, however, as a basis for planning. Locally, the best source of information regarding induction and discharge statistics is generally the Selective Service Board.

The needs of veterans will vary with each individual. Broadly speaking, all discharged men and women will need to shift from military to civilian activity. Many will make the transfer to employment, to school, or other activity without aid from community or government agencies. Friends, relatives, and the ordinary processes of community life will shape their adjustments.

But many veterans will not have friends or relatives to assist them. Many will find the ordinary processes of community life insufficient. Many will be bewildered, restless, perhaps resentful. Some will have physical, mental, emotional handicaps. Many will find no suitable job available. Many will be in new and strange communities.

The discharged man or woman may require counseling on personal or family problems, information, assistance with claims filing and claims prosecution, financial assistance, whether disabled or able-bodied, and financial assistance for dependents, hospitalization, medical and follow-up care, psychiatric and follow-up care, vocational rehabilitation, job training, employment service, unemployment compensation, education, assistance with insurance, help with reassembling the family, guardianship service, farm, home or business loans, and other types of planning. Each man and each woman should have the individual consideration his or her needs require.

For the disabled veteran a broad program of benefits and services is available from the government. Hospitalization for 75,000 veterans of World War I and other wars has been provided. The Veterans Administration now estimates that a bed capacity for 300,000 veterans of this war and previous wars will be needed. With that program will be combined increased services incident to extension of government provisions for hospitalization, unemployment compensation, job placement, education, and loans for business financing or farm or home purchase, as well as broad pension and vocational training benefits. Disabled veterans and dependents of deceased veterans must be guided to these benefits and enabled to avail themselves of those to which they are entitled. Further, in communities throughout the nation, plans should be made for those services, such as mental hygiene facilities, not now generally available.

The "GI Bill of Rights" (The Servicemen's Readjustment Act of 1944, Public Law 346) gives the able-bodied as well as the disabled veteran important new benefits in unemployment compensation, job placement, education, and loans. Able-bodied veterans will be many times more numerous than disabled men or women. They will be competing in jobs with twenty or thirty million displaced war workers. They may require aid after maximum unemployment compensation benefits have been received. Many times they will also need information and guidance.

Not the least important factor is a climate of public understanding warm and healthful to veterans. They will be welcomed and acclaimed upon their return. Outpourings of the home folks and miles of ticker tape will proclaim the gratitude of the nation. Yet not all who shout will know and understand that some returning servicemen have changed in many ways. They are older. Some may be bruised in mind and body. Many may be unsettled. They may be in doubt as to their place in the community. They may bear many of the rough edges, the grime, the tragedy of war. They are not always thus, but many times they are.

The ultimate objective is reabsorption of all veterans into the life of the community and of the nation. Many will return with new experience in leadership and with other experiences and skills which will enable them to make special contributions to the organized life of the community. They will want to participate in their own organizations and in other community and national organizations. Communities and organizations are urged to utilize this new resource and include veterans of this war in their planning councils.

SECTION II. COOPERATIVE PLANNING

THE special problems of the returning serviceman and woman do not differ basically from personal and family situations which always demand a degree of organized social attention. Therefore, the health, welfare, educational, employment, and other types of services required will be basically the same as those now in common use in meeting the social needs of the general population.

Several factors, however, make it inevitable and undoubtedly advisable that the nation, the various states, and the local communities establish special machinery at this time to plan and coordinate services to discharged veterans. They are:

(1) A large group of citizens whose needs for community attention, if any, stem from a single source—their service in the armed forces now exists. In other words, a "category" of need has been created.

(2) Veterans have been recognized as members of a special group by special legislation granting certain privileges.

(3) There is a fairly universal public opinion, based largely on a misconception of the aims and methods of the regular social services, which creates a demand that services to veterans be separated from services to other citizens.

(4) Special agencies, public and private, and special services have been and are being developed for the veteran.

(5) In addition to the normal urge to assist persons with special problems, there are added in this situation the incen-

tives of patriotism and gratitude. This has caused widespread interest in "doing something."

Importance of a Planning and Coordinating Body

Three types of operations are involved in a program to meet the special needs of veterans. It is important to distinguish each from the others. First, there is the job of planning and coordinating made necessary by the great interest in the problem, the importance of the problem, and the variety of services already established or being established. Second, there is the rendering of common services, such as the operation of an information and referral center, which involve the cooperation of all groups. Third, there is the actual administration of direct services to individuals.

The importance of the first of these tasks cannot be overemphasized. A prerequisite to success in handling this problem, whether on the national, state, or local level is the existence of a broadly representative, carefully constituted, and generally accepted committee or central planning body.

The Retraining and Reemployment Administration

The prosecution of war being an operation of the federal government, it is natural that national planning for this war-related problem should center there. On February 24, 1944, the President issued an executive order establishing the Retraining and Reemployment Administration in the Office of War Mobilization. General Frank T. Hines was appointed administrator of this new body, but in an entirely separate capacity from his position as head of the Veterans Administration. The Retraining and Reemployment Administration is a planning and coordinating body and was not established to operate or administer any direct services. The executive order states the function of the RRA to be as follows:

"To have general supervision and direction of the activities of all Government agencies relating to the retraining and reemployment of persons discharged or released from the armed services or other war work, including all work directly affected by the cessation of hostilities or the reduction of the war program; to issue necessary regulations and directions in connection therewith; and to advise with the appropriate committees of the Congress as to the steps taken or to be taken with respect thereto."

The executive order established in connection with the RRA a Retraining and Reemployment Policy Board composed of representatives of the Department of Labor, the Federal Security Agency, the War Manpower Commission, the Selective Service System, the Veterans Administration, the Civil Service Commission, the War Department, the Navy Department, and the War Production Board. One of the activities of this board has been to draw up a statement on information service centers for veterans and war workers. On the basis of this statement by the Policy Board, the RRA issued on May 17, 1944, Order No. 1, covering the organization and operation of veterans' information service centers. This order directs that there shall be established in each state a veterans' service committee composed of representatives of the Selective Service System, the War Manpower Commission, and the Veterans Administration. Also, it is directed that in each community there shall be established a veterans' service committee composed of representatives of the Selective Service System, the United States Employment Service of the War Manpower Commission, and the Veterans Administration insofar as any one or all of these agencies have representatives available in the community. In the case of both the state and local committees, the order provides

· 209 ·

that this official committee may add to its own membership or may represent the federal government on committees of the same nature which have already been established.

In order to provide a channel between local and federal efforts to meet the needs of returning veterans and in order to stimulate and advise local planning efforts, many state governments have already established special commissions or departments. Hundreds of planning groups have come into being locally through the action of city or county governments or under a variety of other auspices. It is apparently the plan of the RRA to work with and through such bodies.

Local Planning

Because every community is different, no two localities will or should set up a veterans' planning body in exactly the same way. The original suggestion that a group should be formed may come from any organization or group or even from an individual citizen leader. The fundamentally important points in connection with this committee are:

(1) That it be representative of organizations rendering service in connection with the problems of veterans.

(2) That there be active participation by able citizen leaders representative of major community points of view and of the principal organizations which have a legitimate interest in planning for the veteran.

(3) That the auspices be such that it will be accepted as the central planning body by all organizations and the public.

(4) That wherever possible paid staff service be made available to assist in carrying out its functions.

(5) That there be only one general planning body.

(6) That it be recognized by and have the cooperation of the local representatives of the RRA.

(7) That in its capacity as a planning body, it not engage in rendering any direct service to individual veterans.

Auspices of Local Planning Body

The following four general types of auspices are suggested, the plan varying according to the peculiar circumstances in each community:

(1) The local veterans' service committee as established by the RRA or by act of an official state planning body.

(2) Local city or county government either by ordinance or by act of the mayor or other official of similar rank in appointing or designating a group to be the official planning body.

(3) Some existing community planning or coordinating group such as a community council, a defense council, a council of social agencies, a Chamber of Commerce, a USO council, a federation of civic groups, or the like.

(4) An independent self-organized group representing a voluntary joining of organizations and citizens for planning and cooperation.

Composition of Local Planning Body

The local planning body may be set up either by having different organizations name delegates or by the appointment of individuals who, because of their interests and organization connections, bring with them different points of view. In most instances the main group will be fairly large and it will be necessary to arrange for the creation of a smaller executive body or committee. A special effort should be made to encourage participation in planning by veterans of the present war.

Following is a list of the types of organizations to be considered which also gives an idea of the range of community interests involved:

(1) Veterans' organizations.

(2) Local offices of state veterans' service departments.

(3) Local offices of federal departments concerned with the problem, including (through the local official veterans' service committee) the Veterans Administration, the United States Employment Service, and the Selective Service System.

(4) Tax-supported and voluntary health, welfare, and recreational agencies and departments.

(5) Industrial and commercial organizations.

(6) Labor organizations.

(7) Religious groups.

(8) Educational groups.

(9) Other clubs and organizations.

Functions of Local Planning Body

The committee should perform the following functions:

(1) Be the central clearing house for all ideas and projects concerning the welfare of the returning veteran to the end that every organization and individual may make the maximum contribution without harmful duplication of effort.

(2) Gather and make available the facts about the number of veterans returning to the community and their potential needs.

(3) Determine the adequacy of direct service facilities to meet the needs of the veteran; plan and stimulate community action for the provision of additional services where necessary; and act as the medium through which organizations rendering services arrive at satisfactory working agreements.

(4) Determine whether or not there is a need for an in-

formation service center and determine the auspices under which it should be administered.

(5) Carry on a program of public interpretation and information regarding the veteran and his proper reception by the community.

(6) Act as the official liaison with state and national veterans' planning bodies.

SECTION III. VETERANS' INFORMATION SERVICE CENTERS

AFTER the formation of a representative planning committee and under its guidance, all governmental and private agencies in each community offering services to veterans, war workers, and their families should participate immediately and actively in the organization of veterans' information service centers where they are needed. The primary purposes of a center would be to inform veterans of the services available to them in the community, to interpret the usefulness of such services, and to refer veterans to the appropriate service agencies. Among the incidental purposes of such a center may be the simplification of referral procedures, the development of cooperation and clarification of function among the service agencies, and the uncovering of gaps in community facilities as a basis for study and action by social planning bodies.

Regardless of how adequate and well organized the public and private welfare organizations in any community may be, experience has shown that the average person knows comparatively little about these agencies and the ways in which he can use them. This is likely to be true particularly with the veteran who returns to his community with a variety of problems which may require the services of several agencies. For this reason, veterans' information service centers began to be organized in many communities in the early months of 1944 to handle inquiries from the large number of men and women being discharged from the armed services. These spontaneous developments showed marked similarity in character even without any concerted guidance through national planning. The development of such centers has now been officially recognized and given guidance by the federal government through Order No. 1 of the Retraining and Reemployment Administration.

Auspices and Organization

The auspices, organization, and program of veterans' information service centers will necessarily vary according to community situations. Large urban communities usually have a variety of service facilities and a relatively effective type of community organization. Small urban communities are, as a rule, less adequately organized and equipped. Some rural areas have little or no organization and few facilities. In any community, however, the development of such a center should be based on joint rather than individual agency planning.

The general responsibility for operation of the center may rest in the general planning body discussed in Section II of this bulletin or that body may wish to place the center under other appropriate auspices such as one of the following:

(1) An already existing governmental planning body such as the local veterans' service committee of the Retraining and Reemployment Administration or a local defense or war-service council.

(2) A new body or committee appointed by the mayor or other local authority, in consultation with the group of interested organizations.

(3) An existing council of social agencies or other quasi-public body, provided its auspices are thoroughly accepted by the broader group.

(4) An appropriate individual agency, selected as the strongest and best equipped, where other auspices are impracticable.

Whatever auspices are selected, however, the center should be under the supervision of a committee or governing body representing community interests. In small communities this supervisory committee may consist of the planning body referred to in Section II of this bulletin, or in large communities it may be created by the group. Such a supervisory committee is equally necessary if the center is operated by a single agency in a small community, in order to avoid a narrowing or specialization of the center's services.

Staffing the Information Service Center

The basic service rendered by the center will be that of providing veterans with information regarding the use of community facilities in meeting personal problems. Therefore, there should be a staff of skilled interviewers with experience in dealing with personal problems and a knowledge of community services in relation to these problems. If possible, interviewers should be professionally trained and experienced social case workers. The following order of preference for the selection of interviewing staff is suggested:

(1) Persons with both experience and professional training.

(2) Persons with professional training but without professional experience.

(3) Persons with actual social work experience but without professional training.

(4) Persons without previous training or experience, but with personal qualities, interests, and attitudes which offer a basis for training in the center itself.

Veterans who are qualified to be interviewers would be an invaluable aid to the success of the center.

It is essential that a professionally trained and experienced social worker be employed as executive, who in addition to handling administrative responsibilities will be able to conduct a staff training program which, depending on the equipment of the group, would place emphasis upon the following:

(1) Development of skill in interviewing.

(2) Knowledge of service-connected problems peculiar to veterans.

(3) Ability to understand and identify a wide range of other personal and family problems.

(4) Detailed knowledge of the services available in the community for each type of problem and of how these services can be used.

(5) Procedures within the center itself.

Depending upon the community situation, the size of staff required, and the resources of the agencies at least a part of the initial interviewing staff may be loaned temporarily by community agencies, but as rapidly as possible such a center should be set up with its own budget and financing and its own employed staff of interviewers.

Services of the Center

The services of the center with the exceptions noted later should be limited to information and referral. Direct services, including treatment, personal counseling, and advice, are primarily the responsibility of the regular service agencies in the community and ordinarily should not be rendered by the center for the following reasons:

(1) They may duplicate and compete with other existing services.

(2) They may lead to a continuing "case load" which will

divert time and attention from the basic information and referral services.

(3) They tend to transform the center into a "treatment" agency with functions which narrow its program.

Services beyond information and referral such as direct medical care, financial assistance and vocational, health and personal counseling and the like, should therefore be the responsibility of appropriate service agencies.

A limited degree of counseling is, of course, involved in giving information and in making referrals to service agencies. Beyond this there may also be certain exceptional situations in which direct counseling in the center may be found necessary, particularly in small or rural communities where the needed service does not exist outside the center. In some communities, the distance or inaccessibility of a service agency may raise a question as to the need or value of a referral, particularly when the counseling required can be completed satisfactorily in one visit to the center. There may also be some acute or emergency problems requiring immediate counseling preceding referral to an appropriate agency.

Where counseling in the center becomes necessary for one of these reasons, it should be recognized as a service distinct from the information and referral process, and entrusted to special personnel trained in the appropriate field such as vocational counseling or health counseling, or case work service. These counselors should, if possible, be placed there by the appropriate agencies. However, where such counseling is undertaken by the center itself because of a lack in the community of the appropriate services, it should be done only in conjunction with efforts in the larger social planning body to develop the needed outside services in the community.

Although the information service centers may be organized primarily for use by discharged servicemen and women, requests for service may come from others in the community, beginning with members of the families of veterans, servicemen on furlough or members of their families, and from war workers and other civilians who need the information the center has to offer. In order to avoid the setting up of several information centers performing the same functions in the community, the veterans' information service center should indicate a readiness to become, or to merge with, a general community information center.

Arrangements with Cooperating Agencies

As early as possible in the development of a center, or in advance, the governing body should have a clear, written understanding with each of the cooperating service agencies covering such points as:

(1) The types of problems which may be referred to the agency, based on the agency's program and competence.

(2) The number of referrals which the agency can handle.

(3) The methods of referral to be used. There should be agreement as to whether the center can accept an application on behalf of the agency, or whether the veteran should be referred to make his own application at the agency's office, or whether the center can promise that the agency will call on the applicant. The National Committee on Service to Veterans believes that the most desirable procedure would probably be for the interviewer at the center to telephone the agency at the conclusion of the interview with the veteran and make an appointment for him with the agency.

Such arrangements should lead to more intelligent use of the services of public and private agencies, avoiding the necessity of refusals of service after referral or of the subsequent "passing on" of referrals from agency to agency. It should be clear, however, that veterans are free to go directly to any agency they choose, without going first to the center, and that such personal applications may be referred directly to another agency where such action is clearly appropriate. The general purpose of the center would be to simplify rather than complicate the use of community services.

The important point to remember is that the usefulness of any centralized information and referral process will depend primarily on the extent to which community services and facilities are available in a cooperative program.

SECTION IV. THE RELATIONSHIP OF COMMUNITY SERVICES TO THE VETERANS' PROGRAM

ALL types of community services will be necessary to the work of information service centers in helping returning servicemen and women make the transition from military to civilian life. Many small communities have few organized social agencies, but all communities have schools, churches, civic organizations, and town or village centers whose active members will willingly provide the necessary contacts and services, sometimes through informal committees which represent their organizations. Larger communities have one or more of the following types of agencies: a family service agency, a Red Cross chapter, a United States Employment Service office, a child care agency, a public welfare agency, a Travelers Aid Society, a YMCA and YWCA, a YM-YWHA, a Catholic agency or other type of community center, and perhaps other health and welfare agencies.

All agencies and organizations interested in and equipped to serve returning members of the armed forces (and war workers) should work together in planning new services, in expanding or adjusting established services, and in furthering civilian understanding of the needs of and service provided for returning veterans and war workers. The agencies can provide a wide range of direct services and some will provide more than one. Each should provide the type of services it is most competent to give. Expansion of any agency's services should be undertaken after conference with the representative and responsible community planning body. New services should be assigned by agreement to the agency best equipped to provide the needed service.

All agencies will stress the importance of a natural and friendly reception to returning servicemen and women. Referrals should be handled quickly and courteously and accurate and up-to-date information about what services can be provided should be readily available.

Counseling, Guidance, Case Work, and Other Services

Men and women will need help ranging from friendly conversation with mature and intelligent workers to social case work and counseling and guidance services dealing with personal problems. Agencies must be cautioned to deal with problems only in the area of their own competence. Interviewers should be carefully selected and trained. Where well-equipped guidance workers and case workers are available, only they should attempt to provide the more skilled professional service required for complicated personal problems. Frequently, the services of physicians or psychiatrists are needed.

Some returning service people will need places to live. Room registries of reasonably priced rooms in homes, clubs, and hotels should be maintained at accessible places in the community. Lists of houses and apartments should be available. YMCA's and YWCA's, YM-YWHA's, and some other community agencies provide housing facilities.

A job will be a first necessity for many returning veterans. The Veterans Personnel Division of the Selective Service System is charged with the legal responsibility of returning discharged servicemen to their old jobs. The United States Employment Service of the War Manpower Commission is responsible for helping veterans secure employment in new jobs. Other community agencies should not attempt to usurp or to duplicate these functions but may find appropriate ways to supplement such services.

Military life will have provided strong group attachments for many men. But the "old crowd" will have disappeared for many who return. Well-planned, varied group activities can help renew old friendships and establish new ones.

Many veterans will have developed new interests while in service at camps and posts, in hospitals, in Red Cross and USO clubs. Opportunities to pursue hobby interests, the crafts, or the arts will appeal to many returning men and women. At community centers and in the community's schools, opportunities can be provided to resume interrupted school work and to seek new training. Formal education for many veterans will be furthered by governmental assistance for tuition and living expenses, but guidance on educational plans may be necessary. Discussion groups and forums, classes in vocational and cultural subjects will attract some.

Churches of all faiths can help many returning men and women reestablish civilian habits of worship and service and to express rediscovered interest in religion. The resources of religious fellowship, of assistance in achieving a philosophy built on religious principles should be readily available.

In all these ways agencies in the community can take a part in helping returning service people and war workers make the necessary, and for many, difficult transition to civilian and postwar living.

SECTION V. FINANCING LOCAL SERVICES

THE financing of auxiliary local services for returning veterans will probably follow the usual local community pattern for financing community services.

In many small communities the expense will be small. Information service centers themselves may be quite informal, with headquarters provided without charge in a municipal building, in the headquarters of a community agency, or in the office or home of a committee chairman. The services of interviewers and other workers, including clerical assistants, may be provided without cost by interested organizations or by the individual workers in the initial stages of the service. Wherever possible, however, funds should be available to employ paid staff for such centers.

No federal funds have been appropriated to finance information service centers, but in some sections state, city, or county funds may be made available. A combination of public and private funds may be secured in some communities.

Both the information service centers and any necessary expansion of related community services can properly be financed through Community War Chests. The regular local community procedures should be followed in requesting such consideration from the Community War Chest. A specific budget should be formulated, including estimates of necessary expenditures and income before presentation to Community War Chests.

SECTION VI. BUILDING PUBLIC UNDERSTANDING

VETERANS are already the most important news item in the national scene, short of the war itself. The problem now is not the amount of publicity, but rather the kind of publicity that will help toward meeting veterans' needs as adequately and in as orderly a way as possible. The importance of what is said and how it is said cannot be overrated because publicity will influence the attitudes of the general community, the veteran's family, his employer, his associates, and himself.

The tone in any publicity about community resources for the returning veterans should be warm but matter-of-fact. It is a perfectly natural situation that in a group of men who have been away from home for a long time and have been in unfamiliar places and circumstances, even if they have not seen actual combat, there will be some who will have special needs when they return. Most of the men, however, will take their places in the community where they left off and it should not be assumed that every veteran will have special problems.

When an information service center is set up, or any type of service for returning veterans is developed, the newspapers will welcome stories and pictures. There will be little trouble in getting the service publicized, because it is news, and "hot" news. Even before a service is set up, the consideration of the veterans' needs by a representative local committee is news.

SOLDIER TO CIVILIAN

Enough of this kind of news has already been published, however, to indicate that there are great dangers to be avoided. in it. Chief among these, in the initial planning stages, is the "Veterans Seen as Big Problem" type of headline and story. A great many newspaper stories printed so far could not fail to lead the community to view with alarm, and with not a little confusion, the prospect of hundreds of khaki-shirted veterans coming home with "problems." It is this kind of publicity which, while it may arouse a community to action, does not always stimulate them to calm and concerted planning. Only too well do we know of the mushrooming of poorly planned, competing services resulting from unwise and hysterical publicity.

A form which this hysteria has been taking in a number of places is an uncoordinated flood of publicity from all kinds of agencies and organizations seeming to compete for the opportunity to serve the veteran. Sometimes these articles ignore the plans of the government and other agencies, giving the impression that the single agency for which they speak offers the only solution to the veterans' problems. To the general public and to the veteran himself these conflicting claims present a very confused picture of community resources. Even when other plans are recognized, publicity describing the work of a specific kind of agency often tends to overemphasize the particular aspect of the veterans' needs with which that agency is prepared to deal. It would be unfortunate, for example, for a mental hygiene agency to describe its services to the psychoneurotic in such a way that the casual reader would assume that most veterans will have psychiatric problems.

It is not necessary that the entire publicity effort in a community be done by one person or one staff. As a matter of fact, it is highly desirable that the publicity resources of all

· 226 ·

agencies be used, because the job is such a large one. It is necessary, however, to coordinate publicity plans on a community-wide basis so that the publicity of each individual organization will be a proper and proportionate part of the total picture.

There is a regrettable tendency on the part of some agencies which are not set up to serve the veteran adequately, or whose programs provide only a minor service to him, to overplay that service in their publicity as a means of getting public attention. Agencies should not use the returning veteran as the theme of their publicity or fund-raising campaigns unless services to him are in truth the theme of their programs also.

Once an agency's plan of services for the returning veteran is clear, the agency wants to make those services known to the veteran and wants to make them known in a way that will make him feel that he is being welcomed back into the community with pleasure, without sentimentality, and without a patronizing, or embarrassing over-solicitousness about his needs and problems. The most common medium through which agencies over the country are considering doing this job of telling the veteran what is available to him in the community is the directory type of booklet. It is not possible, however, to say much about any one service in a directory which covers all of them. Many individual agencies are, therefore, considering the possibility of distributing through information service centers or other central sources fuller statements covering their own services. Even when this is done, however, some balance must be maintained, so that one service, by the amount of its publicity, does not give a false impression of the prevalence of the problem in which it is interested. Only material which is approved by the center should be distributed there.

It is difficult to get much warmth and readability into a directory, and the parts of the directory which are the most difficult to write are those that deal with services for personal problems. It is hard, in a line or two, to define the services of a case work agency, for example, except to those who are already familiar with them and who will know immediately what is meant by "personal problems." Most of the men will not know what kinds of problems a case work agency is prepared to help with and the writer of the directory section dealing with this type of agency must either be completely frank, using such phrases as "If you are having trouble with your wife," or content himself with describing family problems in generalities, which sometimes still leaves the veteran in the dark about what is meant. To strike a happy medium, a balance between the generalization and the too bald listing of distressing personal problems, requires a great deal of skill but is worth the effort.

If the workers in an information service center are thoroughly familiar with the types of service available in the "personal problems" category, then they will be able to interpret these services when they interview a man who seems to be in need of them. This person-to-person interpretation has the great advantage of reaching a specialized audience, whereas printed material for general distribution describing specific kinds of "personal problems" reaches men who do not have the problems and may be puzzled by the apparent assumption that because they are veterans they *must* have problems. In any material of this kind for general distribution, there should be the implication that probably the veteran will settle his own problems satisfactorily, but that if by any chance he wants information and assistance, it is available to him.

Of course, not all publicity directed to the men themselves

will be done through directories, booklets, or direct interviews. Some publicity will reach them through posters, newspapers, radio, and through discussions in various meetings where veterans are the audience. Very important will be the interpretation done by board members, volunteers, and other workers on committees which are working on the services themselves. The principles outlined here, however, apply to all publicity done anywhere and by any medium when it is directed to the men who are the potential users of the services.

Perhaps the most important responsibility which must be faced by those concerned with the speedy and happy readjustment of the veteran to civilian life is the responsibility of helping the community to know how to treat the newly returned veteran. In considering this job of "attitude education" in communities, it must be realized that thousands of men for whom the war is already over are returning to the community now and that a greater proportion of these men have problems of physical or mental readjustment than will those who come home after victory. Unfortunately, the American public has not developed an adequate understanding of the factors in mental health or the psychological strains in the readjustment of the physically disabled. Red Cross hospital workers overseas report that the most prevalent fear of the disabled man who is returning to civilian life is that his family and his community will not understand. He is afraid of too many questions, and afraid that people will stare at him on the streets or tactlessly offer too much help. The veteran who looks hale and hearty even though disabled is disturbed about the way in which he may be received. Communities often fail to understand the veteran who, in his insecurity, takes refuge in overaggressiveness. Well-meaning, warmhearted, American communities do not want to make mistakes with these returning men, but they need help in knowing how to avoid mistakes.

There are dozens of ways in which to tackle the job of "attitude education." Already several towns are having meetings of social workers and health workers to discuss the way veterans feel and want to be treated. One large eastern city has successful and well-attended courses for employers of returned veterans. Organizations whose members are older girls have been sponsoring discussions and club meetings to consider the ways in which the girls, who will be the natural companions of the returning young men, shall conduct themselves toward helping the boys to feel at home and secure. Radio "soap operas," short stories in women's magazines, authoritative articles by psychiatrists and others in the national magazines are all doing their part toward teaching the community to help the veteran with his readjustment wisely. Many of these articles can be reprinted locally as a means of calling the community's attention to them. Local radio stations will be interested in programs which will take up this important subject. One community, for example, reports plans for a local radio series of panel discussions, using psychiatrists and workers from a nearby military hospital as speakers on this newsworthy subject. Women's clubs, church groups, men's service clubs, and all kinds of local organizations should be considered as possible avenues through which qualified people in the community can help to educate citizens about the veteran.

If, in this "attitude education," our matter-of-factness is lost and "problems" are dwelt on too dramatically, there is a danger that by the time the general demobilization comes our communities may be convinced that veterans not only have problems but that they *are* problems. The job of "attitude education" must be done calmly and soundly. After all, the veterans also read the papers and listen to the radio. A good criterion for whether or not publicity is sufficiently dignified and matter-of-fact is to consider what may be the returned veteran's reaction to the material. As a matter of fact, asking returned veterans to cooperate in preparing publicity, letting them see the material, or asking them to attend some of the meetings where it will be easy and natural for them, is an excellent way of being sure that the publicity is on the right track.

MEMBERS OF THE NATIONAL COMMITTEE ON SERVICE TO VETERANS UNDER THE AUSPICES OF THE NATIONAL SOCIAL WORK COUNCIL

ROBERT E. BONDY, *Chairman*
> Administrator, Services to the Armed Forces, American National Red Cross

MRS. SALLIE E. BRIGHT
> Executive Secretary, National Publicity Council for Health and Welfare Services, Inc.

LYMAN S. FORD
> Director, Health and Welfare. Planning, Community Chests and Councils, Inc.

DAVID H. HOLBROOK
> Secretary, National Social Work Council

RAY JOHNS
> Director, Department of Operations, Continental United States, United Service Organizations, Inc.

ROY E. JOHNSON
> Chief, Area Services, Services to the Armed Forces, American National Red Cross

LOUIS KRAFT
> Executive Director, National Jewish Welfare Board

HARRY L. LURIE

Executive Director, Council of Jewish Federations and Welfare Funds

MISS BERTHA MCCALL

General Director, National Travelers Aid Association

RT. REV. JOHN O'GRADY

Secretary, National Conference of Catholic Charities

HOWARD L. RUSSELL

Director, American Public Welfare Association

J. EDWARD SPROUL

Executive for Program Service, National Council of Y.M.C.A.'s; Chairman, National Education-Recreation Council

GEORGE S. STEVENSON, M.D.

Medical Director, National Committee for Mental Hygiene

LINTON B. SWIFT

General Director, Family Welfare Association of America